ISBN 0-8373-2461-0

C-2461   CAREER EXAMINATION SERIES

This is your
PASSBOOK® for...

D1478079

Personnel
Clerk

Test Preparation Study Guide

Questions & Answers

NATIONAL LEARNING CORPORATION

PASSBOOK®
NOTICE

This book is SOLELY intended for, is sold ONLY to, and its use is RESTRICTED to *individual*, bona fide applicants or candidates who qualify by virtue of having seriously filed applications for appropriate license, certificate, professional and/or promotional advancement, higher school matriculation, scholarship, or other legitimate requirements of educational and/or governmental authorities.

This book is NOT intended for use, class instruction, tutoring, training, duplication, copying, reprinting, excerption, or adaptation, etc., by:

(1) Other publishers

(2) Proprietors and/or Instructors of "Coaching" and/or Preparatory Courses

(3) Personnel and/or Training Divisions of commercial, industrial, and governmental organizations

(4) Schools, colleges, or universities and/or their departments and staffs, including teachers and other personnel

(5) Testing Agencies or Bureaus

(6) Study groups which seek by the purchase of a single volume to copy and/or duplicate and/or adapt this material for use by the group as a whole without having purchased individual volumes for each of the members of the group

(7) Et al.

Such persons would be in violation of appropriate Federal and State statutes.

PROVISION OF LICENSING AGREEMENTS. — Recognized educational commercial, industrial, and governmental institutions and organizations, and others legitimately engaged in educational pursuits, including training, testing, and measurement activities, may address a request for a licensing agreement to the copyright owners, who will determine whether, and under what conditions, including fees and charges, the materials in this book may be used by them. In other words, a licensing facility exists for the legitimate use of the material in this book on other than an individual basis. However, it is asseverated and affirmed here that the material in this book *CANNOT* be used without the receipt of the express permission of such a licensing agreement from the Publishers.

NATIONAL LEARNING CORPORATION
212 Michael Drive
Syosset, New York 11791

Inquiries re licensing agreements should be addressed to:
  The President
  National Learning Corporation
  212 Michael Drive
  Syosset, New York 11791

PASSBOOK® SERIES

THE *PASSBOOK® SERIES* has been created to prepare applicants and candidates for the ultimate academic battlefield — the examination room.

At some time in our lives, each and every one of us may be required to take an examination — for validation, matriculation, admission, qualification, registration, certification, or licensure.

Based on the assumption that every applicant or candidate has met the basic formal educational standards, has taken the required number of courses, and read the necessary texts, the *PASSBOOK® SERIES* furnishes the one special preparation which may assure passing with confidence, instead of failing with insecurity. Examination questions — together with answers — are furnished as the basic vehicle for study so that the mysteries of the examination and its compounding difficulties may be eliminated or diminished by a sure method.

This book is meant to help you pass your examination provided that you qualify and are serious in your objective.

The entire field is reviewed through the huge store of content information which is succinctly presented through a provocative and challenging approach — the question-and-answer method.

A climate of success is established by furnishing the correct answers at the end of each test.

You soon learn to recognize types of questions, forms of questions, and patterns of questioning. You may even begin to anticipate expected outcomes.

You perceive that many questions are repeated or adapted so that you can gain acute insights, which may enable you to score many sure points.

You learn how to confront new questions, or types of questions, and to attack them confidently and work out the correct answers.

You note objectives and emphases, and recognize pitfalls and dangers, so that you may make positive educational adjustments.

Moreover, you are kept fully informed in relation to new concepts, methods, practices, and directions in the field.

You discover that you are actually taking the examination all the time: you are preparing for the examination by "taking" an examination, not by reading extraneous and/or supererogatory textbooks.

In short, this PASSBOOK®, used directedly, should be an important factor in helping you to pass your test.

PERSONNEL CLERK

DUTIES
Under direct supervision, performs varied clerical tasks of a routine nature in the processing and maintenance of personnel forms and records. Does related work as required.

SCOPE OF THE EXAMINATION
The written test will cover knowledge, skills and/or abilities in such areas as:
1. Advising and interacting with others;
2. Filing;
3. Office record keeping;
4. Preparing written material; and
5. Understanding and interpreting written material.

HOW TO TAKE A TEST

I. YOU MUST PASS AN EXAMINATION

A. WHAT EVERY CANDIDATE SHOULD KNOW

Examination applicants often ask us for help in preparing for the written test. What can I study in advance? What kinds of questions will be asked? How will the test be given? How will the papers be graded?

As an applicant for a civil service examination, you may be wondering about some of these things. Our purpose here is to suggest effective methods of advance study and to describe civil service examinations.

Your chances for success on this examination can be increased if you know how to prepare. Those "pre-examination jitters" can be reduced if you know what to expect. You can even experience an adventure in good citizenship if you know why civil service exams are given.

B. WHY ARE CIVIL SERVICE EXAMINATIONS GIVEN?

Civil service examinations are important to you in two ways. As a citizen, you want public jobs filled by employees who know how to do their work. As a job seeker, you want a fair chance to compete for that job on an equal footing with other candidates. The best-known means of accomplishing this two-fold goal is the competitive examination.

Exams are widely publicized throughout the nation. They may be administered for jobs in federal, state, city, municipal, town or village governments or agencies.

Any citizen may apply, with some limitations, such as the age or residence of applicants. Your experience and education may be reviewed to see whether you meet the requirements for the particular examination. When these requirements exist, they are reasonable and applied consistently to all applicants. Thus, a competitive examination may cause you some uneasiness now, but it is your privilege and safeguard.

C. HOW ARE CIVIL SERVICE EXAMS DEVELOPED?

Examinations are carefully written by trained technicians who are specialists in the field known as "psychological measurement," in consultation with recognized authorities in the field of work that the test will cover. These experts recommend the subject matter areas or skills to be tested; only those knowledges or skills important to your success on the job are included. The most reliable books and source materials available are used as references. Together, the experts and technicians judge the difficulty level of the questions.

Test technicians know how to phrase questions so that the problem is clearly stated. Their ethics do not permit "trick" or "catch" questions. Questions may have been tried out on sample groups, or subjected to statistical analysis, to determine their usefulness.

Written tests are often used in combination with performance tests, ratings of training and experience, and oral interviews. All of these measures combine to form the best-known means of finding the right person for the right job.

II. HOW TO PASS THE WRITTEN TEST

A. NATURE OF THE EXAMINATION

To prepare intelligently for civil service examinations, you should know how they differ from school examinations you have taken. In school you were assigned certain definite pages to read or subjects to cover. The examination questions were quite detailed and usually emphasized memory. Civil service exams, on the other hand, try to discover your present ability to perform the duties of a position, plus your potentiality to learn these duties. In other words, a civil service exam attempts to predict how successful you will be. Questions cover such a broad area that they cannot be as minute and detailed as school exam questions.

In the public service similar kinds of work, or positions, are grouped together in one "class." This process is known as *position-classification*. All the positions in a class are paid according to the salary range for that class. One class title covers all of these positions, and they are all tested by the same examination.

B. FOUR BASIC STEPS

1) Study the announcement

How, then, can you know what subjects to study? Our best answer is: "Learn as much as possible about the class of positions for which you've applied." The exam will test the knowledge, skills and abilities needed to do the work.

Your most valuable source of information about the position you want is the official exam announcement. This announcement lists the training and experience qualifications. Check these standards and apply only if you come reasonably close to meeting them.

The brief description of the position in the examination announcement offers some clues to the subjects which will be tested. Think about the job itself. Review the duties in your mind. Can you perform them, or are there some in which you are rusty? Fill in the blank spots in your preparation.

Many jurisdictions preview the written test in the exam announcement by including a section called "Knowledge and Abilities Required," "Scope of the Examination," or some similar heading. Here you will find out specifically what fields will be tested.

2) Review your own background

Once you learn in general what the position is all about, and what you need to know to do the work, ask yourself which subjects you already know fairly well and which need improvement. You may wonder whether to concentrate on improving your strong areas or on building some background in your fields of weakness. When the announcement has specified "some knowledge" or "considerable knowledge," or has used adjectives like "beginning principles of..." or "advanced ... methods," you can get a clue as to the number and difficulty of questions to be asked in any given field. More questions, and hence broader coverage, would be included for those subjects which are more important in the work. Now weigh your strengths and weaknesses against the job requirements and prepare accordingly.

3) Determine the level of the position

Another way to tell how intensively you should prepare is to understand the level of the job for which you are applying. Is it the entering level? In other words, is this the position in which beginners in a field of work are hired? Or is it an intermediate or advanced level? Sometimes this is indicated by such words as "Junior" or "Senior" in the class title. Other jurisdictions use Roman numerals to designate the level – Clerk I, Clerk II, for example. The word "Supervisor" sometimes appears in the title. If the level is not indicated by the title, check the description of duties. Will you be working under very close supervision, or will you have responsibility for independent decisions in this work?

4) Choose appropriate study materials

Now that you know the subjects to be examined and the relative amount of each subject to be covered, you can choose suitable study materials. For beginning level jobs, or even advanced ones, if you have a pronounced weakness in some aspect of your training, read a modern, standard textbook in that field. Be sure it is up to date and has general coverage. Such books are normally available at your library, and the librarian will be glad to help you locate one. For entry-level positions, questions of appropriate difficulty are chosen – neither highly advanced questions, nor those too simple. Such questions require careful thought but not advanced training.

If the position for which you are applying is technical or advanced, you will read more advanced, specialized material. If you are already familiar with the basic principles of your field, elementary textbooks would waste your time. Concentrate on advanced textbooks and technical periodicals. Think through the concepts and review difficult problems in your field.

These are all general sources. You can get more ideas on your own initiative, following these leads. For example, training manuals and publications of the government agency which employs workers in your field can be useful, particularly for technical and professional positions. A letter or visit to the government department involved may result in more specific study suggestions, and certainly will provide you with a more definite idea of the exact nature of the position you are seeking.

III. KINDS OF TESTS

Tests are used for purposes other than measuring knowledge and ability to perform specified duties. For some positions, it is equally important to test ability to make adjustments to new situations or to profit from training. In others, basic mental abilities not dependent on information are essential. Questions which test these things may not appear as pertinent to the duties of the position as those which test for knowledge and information. Yet they are often highly important parts of a fair examination. For very general questions, it is almost impossible to help you direct your study efforts. What we can do is to point out some of the more common of these general abilities needed in public service positions and describe some typical questions.

1) General information

Broad, general information has been found useful for predicting job success in some kinds of work. This is tested in a variety of ways, from vocabulary lists to questions about current events. Basic background in some field of work, such as sociology or economics, may be sampled in a group of questions. Often these are principles which have become familiar to most persons through exposure rather than through formal training. It is difficult to advise you how to study for these questions; being alert to the world around you is our best suggestion.

2) Verbal ability

An example of an ability needed in many positions is verbal or language ability. Verbal ability is, in brief, the ability to use and understand words. Vocabulary and grammar tests are typical measures of this ability. Reading comprehension or paragraph interpretation questions are common in many kinds of civil service tests. You are given a paragraph of written material and asked to find its central meaning.

3) Numerical ability

Number skills can be tested by the familiar arithmetic problem, by checking paired lists of numbers to see which are alike and which are different, or by interpreting charts and graphs. In the latter test, a graph may be printed in the test booklet which you are asked to use as the basis for answering questions.

4) Observation

A popular test for law-enforcement positions is the observation test. A picture is shown to you for several minutes, then taken away. Questions about the picture test your ability to observe both details and larger elements.

5) Following directions

In many positions in the public service, the employee must be able to carry out written instructions dependably and accurately. You may be given a chart with several columns, each column listing a variety of information. The questions require you to carry out directions involving the information given in the chart.

6) Skills and aptitudes

Performance tests effectively measure some manual skills and aptitudes. When the skill is one in which you are trained, such as typing or shorthand, you can practice. These tests are often very much like those given in business school or high school courses. For many of the other skills and aptitudes, however, no short-time preparation can be made. Skills and abilities natural to you or that you have developed throughout your lifetime are being tested.

Many of the general questions just described provide all the data needed to answer the questions and ask you to use your reasoning ability to find the answers. Your best preparation for these tests, as well as for tests of facts and ideas, is to be at your physical and mental best. You, no doubt, have your own methods of getting into an exam-taking mood and keeping "in shape." The next section lists some ideas on this subject.

IV. KINDS OF QUESTIONS

Only rarely is the "essay" question, which you answer in narrative form, used in civil service tests. Civil service tests are usually of the short-answer type. Full instructions for answering these questions will be given to you at the examination. But in case this is your first experience with short-answer questions and separate answer sheets, here is what you need to know:

1) Multiple-choice Questions

Most popular of the short-answer questions is the "multiple choice" or "best answer" question. It can be used, for example, to test for factual knowledge, ability to solve problems or judgment in meeting situations found at work.

A multiple-choice question is normally one of three types—

- It can begin with an incomplete statement followed by several possible endings. You are to find the one ending which *best* completes the statement, although some of the others may not be entirely wrong.
- It can also be a complete statement in the form of a question which is answered by choosing one of the statements listed.

- It can be in the form of a problem – again you select the best answer.

Here is an example of a multiple-choice question with a discussion which should give you some clues as to the method for choosing the right answer:

When an employee has a complaint about his assignment, the action which will *best* help him overcome his difficulty is to
- A. discuss his difficulty with his coworkers
- B. take the problem to the head of the organization
- C. take the problem to the person who gave him the assignment
- D. say nothing to anyone about his complaint

In answering this question, you should study each of the choices to find which is best. Consider choice "A" – Certainly an employee may discuss his complaint with fellow employees, but no change or improvement can result, and the complaint remains unresolved. Choice "B" is a poor choice since the head of the organization probably does not know what assignment you have been given, and taking your problem to him is known as "going over the head" of the supervisor. The supervisor, or person who made the assignment, is the person who can clarify it or correct any injustice. Choice "C" is, therefore, correct. To say nothing, as in choice "D," is unwise. Supervisors have and interest in knowing the problems employees are facing, and the employee is seeking a solution to his problem.

2) True/False Questions

The "true/false" or "right/wrong" form of question is sometimes used. Here a complete statement is given. Your job is to decide whether the statement is right or wrong.

SAMPLE: A roaming cell-phone call to a nearby city costs less than a non-roaming call to a distant city.

This statement is wrong, or false, since roaming calls are more expensive.

This is not a complete list of all possible question forms, although most of the others are variations of these common types. You will always get complete directions for answering questions. Be sure you understand *how* to mark your answers – ask questions until you do.

V. RECORDING YOUR ANSWERS

Computer terminals are used more and more today for many different kinds of exams.

For an examination with very few applicants, you may be told to record your answers in the test booklet itself. Separate answer sheets are much more common. If this separate answer sheet is to be scored by machine – and this is often the case – it is highly important that you mark your answers correctly in order to get credit.

An electronic scoring machine is often used in civil service offices because of the speed with which papers can be scored. Machine-scored answer sheets must be marked with a pencil, which will be given to you. This pencil has a high graphite content which responds to the electronic scoring machine. As a matter of fact, stray dots may register as answers, so do not let your pencil rest on the answer sheet while you are pondering the correct answer. Also, if your pencil lead breaks or is otherwise defective, ask for another.

Since the answer sheet will be dropped in a slot in the scoring machine, be careful not to bend the corners or get the paper crumpled.

The answer sheet normally has five vertical columns of numbers, with 30 numbers to a column. These numbers correspond to the question numbers in your test booklet. After each number, going across the page are four or five pairs of dotted lines. These short dotted lines have small letters or numbers above them. The first two pairs may also have a "T" or "F" above the letters. This indicates that the first two pairs only are to be used if the questions are of the true-false type. If the questions are multiple choice, disregard the "T" and "F" and pay attention only to the small letters or numbers.

Answer your questions in the manner of the sample that follows:

32. The largest city in the United States is
   A. Washington, D.C.
   B. New York City
   C. Chicago
   D. Detroit
   E. San Francisco

1) Choose the answer you think is best. (New York City is the largest, so "B" is correct.)
2) Find the row of dotted lines numbered the same as the question you are answering. (Find row number 32)
3) Find the pair of dotted lines corresponding to the answer. (Find the pair of lines under the mark "B.")
4) Make a solid black mark between the dotted lines.

VI. BEFORE THE TEST

Common sense will help you find procedures to follow to get ready for an examination. Too many of us, however, overlook these sensible measures. Indeed, nervousness and fatigue have been found to be the most serious reasons why applicants fail to do their best on civil service tests. Here is a list of reminders:

• Begin your preparation early – Don't wait until the last minute to go scurrying around for books and materials or to find out what the position is all about.
• Prepare continuously – An hour a night for a week is better than an all-night cram session. This has been definitely established. What is more, a night a week for a month will return better dividends than crowding your study into a shorter period of time.
• Locate the place of the exam – You have been sent a notice telling you when and where to report for the examination. If the location is in a different town or otherwise unfamiliar to you, it would be well to inquire the best route and learn something about the building.
• Relax the night before the test – Allow your mind to rest. Do not study at all that night. Plan some mild recreation or diversion; then go to bed early and get a good night's sleep.
• Get up early enough to make a leisurely trip to the place for the test – This way unforeseen events, traffic snarls, unfamiliar buildings, etc. will not upset you.
• Dress comfortably – A written test is not a fashion show. You will be known by number and not by name, so wear something comfortable.

- Leave excess paraphernalia at home – Shopping bags and odd bundles will get in your way. You need bring only the items mentioned in the official notice you received; usually everything you need is provided. Do not bring reference books to the exam. They will only confuse those last minutes and be taken away from you when in the test room.
- Arrive somewhat ahead of time – If because of transportation schedules you must get there very early, bring a newspaper or magazine to take your mind off yourself while waiting.
- Locate the examination room – When you have found the proper room, you will be directed to the seat or part of the room where you will sit. Sometimes you are given a sheet of instructions to read while you are waiting. Do not fill out any forms until you are told to do so; just read them and be prepared.
- Relax and prepare to listen to the instructions
- If you have any physical problem that may keep you from doing your best, be sure to tell the test administrator. If you are sick or in poor health, you really cannot do your best on the exam. You can come back and take the test some other time.

VII. AT THE TEST

The day of the test is here and you have the test booklet in your hand. The temptation to get going is very strong. Caution! There is more to success than knowing the right answers. You must know how to identify your papers and understand variations in the type of short-answer question used in this particular examination. Follow these suggestions for maximum results from your efforts:

1) Cooperate with the monitor
The test administrator has a duty to create a situation in which you can be as much at ease as possible. He will give instructions, tell you when to begin, check to see that you are marking your answer sheet correctly, and so on. He is not there to guard you, although he will see that your competitors do not take unfair advantage. He wants to help you do your best.

2) Listen to all instructions
Don't jump the gun! Wait until you understand all directions. In most civil service tests you get more time than you need to answer the questions. So don't be in a hurry. Read each word of instructions until you clearly understand the meaning. Study the examples, listen to all announcements and follow directions. Ask questions if you do not understand what to do.

3) Identify your papers
Civil service exams are usually identified by number only. You will be assigned a number; you must not put your name on your test papers. Be sure to copy your number correctly. Since more than one exam may be given, copy your exact examination title.

4) Plan your time
Unless you are told that a test is a "speed" or "rate of work" test, speed itself is usually not important. Time enough to answer all the questions will be provided, but this does not mean that you have all day. An overall time limit has been set. Divide the total time (in minutes) by the number of questions to determine the approximate time you have for each question.

5) Do not linger over difficult questions

If you come across a difficult question, mark it with a paper clip (useful to have along) and come back to it when you have been through the booklet. One caution if you do this – be sure to skip a number on your answer sheet as well. Check often to be sure that you have not lost your place and that you are marking in the row numbered the same as the question you are answering.

6) Read the questions

Be sure you know what the question asks! Many capable people are unsuccessful because they failed to *read* the questions correctly.

7) Answer all questions

Unless you have been instructed that a penalty will be deducted for incorrect answers, it is better to guess than to omit a question.

8) Speed tests

It is often better NOT to guess on speed tests. It has been found that on timed tests people are tempted to spend the last few seconds before time is called in marking answers at random – without even reading them – in the hope of picking up a few extra points. To discourage this practice, the instructions may warn you that your score will be "corrected" for guessing. That is, a penalty will be applied. The incorrect answers will be deducted from the correct ones, or some other penalty formula will be used.

9) Review your answers

If you finish before time is called, go back to the questions you guessed or omitted to give them further thought. Review other answers if you have time.

10) Return your test materials

If you are ready to leave before others have finished or time is called, take ALL your materials to the monitor and leave quietly. Never take any test material with you. The monitor can discover whose papers are not complete, and taking a test booklet may be grounds for disqualification.

VIII. EXAMINATION TECHNIQUES

1) Read the general instructions carefully. These are usually printed on the first page of the exam booklet. As a rule, these instructions refer to the timing of the examination; the fact that you should not start work until the signal and must stop work at a signal, etc. If there are any *special* instructions, such as a choice of questions to be answered, make sure that you note this instruction carefully.

2) When you are ready to start work on the examination, that is as soon as the signal has been given, read the instructions to each question booklet, underline any key words or phrases, such as *least, best, outline, describe* and the like. In this way you will tend to answer as requested rather than discover on reviewing your paper that you *listed without describing*, that you selected the *worst* choice rather than the *best* choice, etc.

3) If the examination is of the objective or multiple-choice type – that is, each question will also give a series of possible answers: A, B, C or D, and you are called upon to select the best answer and write the letter next to that answer on your answer paper – it is advisable to start answering each question in turn. There may be anywhere from 50 to 100 such questions in the three or four hours allotted and you can see how much time would be taken if you read through all the questions before beginning to answer any. Furthermore, if you come across a question or group of questions which you know would be difficult to answer, it would undoubtedly affect your handling of all the other questions.

4) If the examination is of the essay type and contains but a few questions, it is a moot point as to whether you should read all the questions before starting to answer any one. Of course, if you are given a choice – say five out of seven and the like – then it is essential to read all the questions so you can eliminate the two that are most difficult. If, however, you are asked to answer all the questions, there may be danger in trying to answer the easiest one first because you may find that you will spend too much time on it. The best technique is to answer the first question, then proceed to the second, etc.

5) Time your answers. Before the exam begins, write down the time it started, then add the time allowed for the examination and write down the time it must be completed, then divide the time available somewhat as follows:
   - If 3-1/2 hours are allowed, that would be 210 minutes. If you have 80 objective-type questions, that would be an average of 2-1/2 minutes per question. Allow yourself no more than 2 minutes per question, or a total of 160 minutes, which will permit about 50 minutes to review.
   - If for the time allotment of 210 minutes there are 7 essay questions to answer, that would average about 30 minutes a question. Give yourself only 25 minutes per question so that you have about 35 minutes to review.

6) The most important instruction is to *read each question* and make sure you know what is wanted. The second most important instruction is to *time yourself properly* so that you answer every question. The third most important instruction is to *answer every question*. Guess if you have to but include something for each question. Remember that you will receive no credit for a blank and will probably receive some credit if you write something in answer to an essay question. If you guess a letter – say "B" for a multiple-choice question – you may have guessed right. If you leave a blank as an answer to a multiple-choice question, the examiners may respect your feelings but it will not add a point to your score. Some exams may penalize you for wrong answers, so in such cases *only*, you may not want to guess unless you have some basis for your answer.

7) Suggestions
   a. Objective-type questions
      1. Examine the question booklet for proper sequence of pages and questions
      2. Read all instructions carefully
      3. Skip any question which seems too difficult; return to it after all other questions have been answered
      4. Apportion your time properly; do not spend too much time on any single question or group of questions

5. Note and underline key words – *all, most, fewest, least, best, worst, same, opposite,* etc.
6. Pay particular attention to negatives
7. Note unusual option, e.g., unduly long, short, complex, different or similar in content to the body of the question
8. Observe the use of "hedging" words – *probably, may, most likely,* etc.
9. Make sure that your answer is put next to the same number as the question
10. Do not second-guess unless you have good reason to believe the second answer is definitely more correct
11. Cross out original answer if you decide another answer is more accurate; do not erase until you are ready to hand your paper in
12. Answer all questions; guess unless instructed otherwise
13. Leave time for review

  b. Essay questions
    1. Read each question carefully
    2. Determine exactly what is wanted. Underline key words or phrases.
    3. Decide on outline or paragraph answer
    4. Include many different points and elements unless asked to develop any one or two points or elements
    5. Show impartiality by giving pros and cons unless directed to select one side only
    6. Make and write down any assumptions you find necessary to answer the questions
    7. Watch your English, grammar, punctuation and choice of words
    8. Time your answers; don't crowd material

8) Answering the essay question

Most essay questions can be answered by framing the specific response around several key words or ideas. Here are a few such key words or ideas:

M's: manpower, materials, methods, money, management
P's: purpose, program, policy, plan, procedure, practice, problems, pitfalls, personnel, public relations
  a. Six basic steps in handling problems:
    1. Preliminary plan and background development
    2. Collect information, data and facts
    3. Analyze and interpret information, data and facts
    4. Analyze and develop solutions as well as make recommendations
    5. Prepare report and sell recommendations
    6. Install recommendations and follow up effectiveness

  b. Pitfalls to avoid
    1. *Taking things for granted* – A statement of the situation does not necessarily imply that each of the elements is necessarily true; for example, a complaint may be invalid and biased so that all that can be taken for granted is that a complaint has been registered

2. *Considering only one side of a situation* – Wherever possible, indicate several alternatives and then point out the reasons you selected the best one
3. *Failing to indicate follow up* – Whenever your answer indicates action on your part, make certain that you will take proper follow-up action to see how successful your recommendations, procedures or actions turn out to be
4. *Taking too long in answering any single question* – Remember to time your answers properly

IX. AFTER THE TEST

Scoring procedures differ in detail among civil service jurisdictions although the general principles are the same. Whether the papers are hand-scored or graded by machine we have described, they are nearly always graded by number. That is, the person who marks the paper knows only the number – never the name – of the applicant. Not until all the papers have been graded will they be matched with names. If other tests, such as training and experience or oral interview ratings have been given, scores will be combined. Different parts of the examination usually have different weights. For example, the written test might count 60 percent of the final grade, and a rating of training and experience 40 percent. In many jurisdictions, veterans will have a certain number of points added to their grades.

After the final grade has been determined, the names are placed in grade order and an eligible list is established. There are various methods for resolving ties between those who get the same final grade – probably the most common is to place first the name of the person whose application was received first. Job offers are made from the eligible list in the order the names appear on it. You will be notified of your grade and your rank as soon as all these computations have been made. This will be done as rapidly as possible.

People who are found to meet the requirements in the announcement are called "eligibles." Their names are put on a list of eligible candidates. An eligible's chances of getting a job depend on how high he stands on this list and how fast agencies are filling jobs from the list.

When a job is to be filled from a list of eligibles, the agency asks for the names of people on the list of eligibles for that job. When the civil service commission receives this request, it sends to the agency the names of the three people highest on this list. Or, if the job to be filled has specialized requirements, the office sends the agency the names of the top three persons who meet these requirements from the general list.

The appointing officer makes a choice from among the three people whose names were sent to him. If the selected person accepts the appointment, the names of the others are put back on the list to be considered for future openings.

That is the rule in hiring from all kinds of eligible lists, whether they are for typist, carpenter, chemist, or something else. For every vacancy, the appointing officer has his choice of any one of the top three eligibles on the list. This explains why the person whose name is on top of the list sometimes does not get an appointment when some of the persons lower on the list do. If the appointing officer chooses the second or third eligible, the No. 1 eligible does not get a job at once, but stays on the list until he is appointed or the list is terminated.

X. HOW TO PASS THE INTERVIEW TEST

The examination for which you applied requires an oral interview test. You have already taken the written test and you are now being called for the interview test – the final part of the formal examination.

You may think that it is not possible to prepare for an interview test and that there are no procedures to follow during an interview. Our purpose is to point out some things you can do in advance that will help you and some good rules to follow and pitfalls to avoid while you are being interviewed.

What is an interview supposed to test?

The written examination is designed to test the technical knowledge and competence of the candidate; the oral is designed to evaluate intangible qualities, not readily measured otherwise, and to establish a list showing the relative fitness of each candidate – as measured against his competitors – for the position sought. Scoring is not on the basis of "right" and "wrong," but on a sliding scale of values ranging from "not passable" to "outstanding." As a matter of fact, it is possible to achieve a relatively low score without a single "incorrect" answer because of evident weakness in the qualities being measured.

Occasionally, an examination may consist entirely of an oral test – either an individual or a group oral. In such cases, information is sought concerning the technical knowledges and abilities of the candidate, since there has been no written examination for this purpose. More commonly, however, an oral test is used to supplement a written examination.

Who conducts interviews?

The composition of oral boards varies among different jurisdictions. In nearly all, a representative of the personnel department serves as chairman. One of the members of the board may be a representative of the department in which the candidate would work. In some cases, "outside experts" are used, and, frequently, a businessman or some other representative of the general public is asked to serve. Labor and management or other special groups may be represented. The aim is to secure the services of experts in the appropriate field.

However the board is composed, it is a good idea (and not at all improper or unethical) to ascertain in advance of the interview who the members are and what groups they represent. When you are introduced to them, you will have some idea of their backgrounds and interests, and at least you will not stutter and stammer over their names.

What should be done before the interview?

While knowledge about the board members is useful and takes some of the surprise element out of the interview, there is other preparation which is more substantive. It *is* possible to prepare for an oral interview – in several ways:

1) Keep a copy of your application and review it carefully before the interview

This may be the only document before the oral board, and the starting point of the interview. Know what education and experience you have listed there, and the sequence and dates of all of it. Sometimes the board will ask you to review the highlights of your experience for them; you should not have to hem and haw doing it.

2) Study the class specification and the examination announcement

Usually, the oral board has one or both of these to guide them. The qualities, characteristics or knowledges required by the position sought are stated in these documents. They offer valuable clues as to the nature of the oral interview. For example, if the job involves supervisory responsibilities, the announcement will usually indicate that knowledge of modern supervisory methods and the qualifications of the candidate as a supervisor will be tested. If so, you can expect such questions, frequently in the form of a hypothetical situation which you are expected to solve. NEVER go into an oral without knowledge of the duties and responsibilities of the job you seek.

3) Think through each qualification required

Try to visualize the kind of questions you would ask if you were a board member. How well could you answer them? Try especially to appraise your own knowledge and background in each area, *measured against the job sought*, and identify any areas in which you are weak. Be critical and realistic – do not flatter yourself.

4) Do some general reading in areas in which you feel you may be weak

For example, if the job involves supervision and your past experience has NOT, some general reading in supervisory methods and practices, particularly in the field of human relations, might be useful. Do NOT study agency procedures or detailed manuals. The oral board will be testing your understanding and capacity, not your memory.

5) Get a good night's sleep and watch your general health and mental attitude

You will want a clear head at the interview. Take care of a cold or any other minor ailment, and of course, no hangovers.

What should be done on the day of the interview?

Now comes the day of the interview itself. Give yourself plenty of time to get there. Plan to arrive somewhat ahead of the scheduled time, particularly if your appointment is in the fore part of the day. If a previous candidate fails to appear, the board might be ready for you a bit early. By early afternoon an oral board is almost invariably behind schedule if there are many candidates, and you may have to wait. Take along a book or magazine to read, or your application to review, but leave any extraneous material in the waiting room when you go in for your interview. In any event, relax and compose yourself.

The matter of dress is important. The board is forming impressions about you – from your experience, your manners, your attitude, and your appearance. Give your personal appearance careful attention. Dress your best, but not your flashiest. Choose conservative, appropriate clothing, and be sure it is immaculate. This is a business interview, and your appearance should indicate that you regard it as such. Besides, being well groomed and properly dressed will help boost your confidence.

Sooner or later, someone will call your name and escort you into the interview room. *This is it.* From here on you are on your own. It is too late for any more preparation. But remember, you asked for this opportunity to prove your fitness, and you are here because your request was granted.

What happens when you go in?

The usual sequence of events will be as follows: The clerk (who is often the board stenographer) will introduce you to the chairman of the oral board, who will introduce you to the other members of the board. Acknowledge the introductions before you sit down. Do not be surprised if you find a microphone facing you or a stenotypist sitting by. Oral interviews are usually recorded in the event of an appeal or other review.

Usually the chairman of the board will open the interview by reviewing the highlights of your education and work experience from your application – primarily for the benefit of the other members of the board, as well as to get the material into the record. Do not interrupt or comment unless there is an error or significant misinterpretation; if that is the case, do not hesitate. But do not quibble about insignificant matters. Also, he will usually ask you some question about your education, experience or your present job – partly to get you to start talking and to establish the interviewing "rapport." He may start the actual questioning, or turn it over to one of the other members. Frequently, each member undertakes the questioning on a particular area, one in which he is perhaps most competent, so you can expect each member to participate in the examination. Because time is limited, you may also expect some rather abrupt switches in the direction the questioning takes, so do not be upset by it. Normally, a board member will not pursue a single line of questioning unless he discovers a particular strength or weakness.

After each member has participated, the chairman will usually ask whether any member has any further questions, then will ask you if you have anything you wish to add. Unless you are expecting this question, it may floor you. Worse, it may start you off on an extended, extemporaneous speech. The board is not usually seeking more information. The question is principally to offer you a last opportunity to present further qualifications or to indicate that you have nothing to add. So, if you feel that a significant qualification or characteristic has been overlooked, it is proper to point it out in a sentence or so. Do not compliment the board on the thoroughness of their examination – they have been sketchy, and you know it. If you wish, merely say, "No thank you, I have nothing further to add." This is a point where you can "talk yourself out" of a good impression or fail to present an important bit of information. Remember, *you close the interview yourself.*

The chairman will then say, "That is all, Mr. _____, thank you." Do not be startled; the interview is over, and quicker than you think. Thank him, gather your belongings and take your leave. Save your sigh of relief for the other side of the door.

How to put your best foot forward

Throughout this entire process, you may feel that the board individually and collectively is trying to pierce your defenses, seek out your hidden weaknesses and embarrass and confuse you. Actually, this is not true. They are obliged to make an appraisal of your qualifications for the job you are seeking, and they want to see you in your best light. Remember, they must interview all candidates and a non-cooperative candidate may become a failure in spite of their best efforts to bring out his qualifications. Here are 15 suggestions that will help you:

1) Be natural – Keep your attitude confident, not cocky

If you are not confident that you can do the job, do not expect the board to be. Do not apologize for your weaknesses, try to bring out your strong points. The board is interested in a positive, not negative, presentation. Cockiness will antagonize any board member and make him wonder if you are covering up a weakness by a false show of strength.

2) Get comfortable, but don't lounge or sprawl

Sit erectly but not stiffly. A careless posture may lead the board to conclude that you are careless in other things, or at least that you are not impressed by the importance of the occasion. Either conclusion is natural, even if incorrect. Do not fuss with your clothing, a pencil or an ashtray. Your hands may occasionally be useful to emphasize a point; do not let them become a point of distraction.

3) Do not wisecrack or make small talk

This is a serious situation, and your attitude should show that you consider it as such. Further, the time of the board is limited – they do not want to waste it, and neither should you.

4) Do not exaggerate your experience or abilities

In the first place, from information in the application or other interviews and sources, the board may know more about you than you think. Secondly, you probably will not get away with it. An experienced board is rather adept at spotting such a situation, so do not take the chance.

5) If you know a board member, do not make a point of it, yet do not hide it

Certainly you are not fooling him, and probably not the other members of the board. Do not try to take advantage of your acquaintanceship – it will probably do you little good.

6) Do not dominate the interview

Let the board do that. They will give you the clues – do not assume that you have to do all the talking. Realize that the board has a number of questions to ask you, and do not try to take up all the interview time by showing off your extensive knowledge of the answer to the first one.

7) Be attentive

You only have 20 minutes or so, and you should keep your attention at its sharpest throughout. When a member is addressing a problem or question to you, give him your undivided attention. Address your reply principally to him, but do not exclude the other board members.

8) Do not interrupt

A board member may be stating a problem for you to analyze. He will ask you a question when the time comes. Let him state the problem, and wait for the question.

9) Make sure you understand the question

Do not try to answer until you are sure what the question is. If it is not clear, restate it in your own words or ask the board member to clarify it for you. However, do not haggle about minor elements.

10) Reply promptly but not hastily

A common entry on oral board rating sheets is "candidate responded readily," or "candidate hesitated in replies." Respond as promptly and quickly as you can, but do not jump to a hasty, ill-considered answer.

11) Do not be peremptory in your answers

A brief answer is proper – but do not fire your answer back. That is a losing game from your point of view. The board member can probably ask questions much faster than you can answer them.

12) Do not try to create the answer you think the board member wants

He is interested in what kind of mind you have and how it works – not in playing games. Furthermore, he can usually spot this practice and will actually grade you down on it.

13) Do not switch sides in your reply merely to agree with a board member

Frequently, a member will take a contrary position merely to draw you out and to see if you are willing and able to defend your point of view. Do not start a debate, yet do not surrender a good position. If a position is worth taking, it is worth defending.

14) Do not be afraid to admit an error in judgment if you are shown to be wrong

   The board knows that you are forced to reply without any opportunity for careful consideration. Your answer may be demonstrably wrong. If so, admit it and get on with the interview.

15) Do not dwell at length on your present job

   The opening question may relate to your present assignment. Answer the question but do not go into an extended discussion. You are being examined for a *new* job, not your present one. As a matter of fact, try to phrase ALL your answers in terms of the job for which you are being examined.

Basis of Rating

   Probably you will forget most of these "do's" and "don'ts" when you walk into the oral interview room. Even remembering them all will not ensure you a passing grade. Perhaps you did not have the qualifications in the first place. But remembering them will help you to put your best foot forward, without treading on the toes of the board members.

   Rumor and popular opinion to the contrary notwithstanding, an oral board wants you to make the best appearance possible. They know you are under pressure – but they also want to see how you respond to it as a guide to what your reaction would be under the pressures of the job you seek. They will be influenced by the degree of poise you display, the personal traits you show and the manner in which you respond.

ABOUT THIS BOOK

   This book contains tests, divided into Examination Sections. Go through each test, answering every question in the margin. We have also attached a sample answer sheet at the back of the book that can be removed and used. At the end of each test look at the answer key and check your answers. On the ones you got wrong, look at the right answer choice and learn. Do not fill in the answers first. Do not memorize the questions and answers, but understand the answer and principles involved. On your test, the questions will likely be different from the samples. Questions are changed and new ones added. If you understand these past questions you should have success with any changes that arise. Tests may consist of several types of questions. We have additional books on each subject should more study be advisable or necessary for you. Finally, the more you study, the better prepared you will be. This book is intended to be the last thing you study before you walk into the examination room. Prior study of relevant texts is also recommended. NLC published some of these in our Fundamental Series. Knowledge and good sense are important factors in passing your exam. Good luck also helps. So now study this Passbook, absorb the material contained within and take that knowledge into the examination. Then do your best to pass that exam.

EXAMINATION SECTION

EXAMINATION SECTION
TEST 1

DIRECTIONS: Each question or incomplete statement is followed by several suggested answers or completions. Select the one that BEST answers the question or completes the statement. *PRINT THE LETTER OF THE CORRECT ANSWER IN THE SPACE AT THE RIGHT.*

1. Assume that you have been assigned by your supervisor to file some record cards in a cabinet. All the cards in this cabinet are supposed to be kept in strict alphabetical order. You know that important work is being held up because certain cards in this cabinet cannot be located. While filing the records given you, you come across a card which is not in its correct alphabetical place.
   Of the following, the BEST reason for you to bring this record to the attention of your supervisor is that

    1.____

    A. errors in filing are more serious than other types of errors
    B. your alertness in locating the card should be rewarded
    C. the filing system may be at fault, rather than the employee who misfiled the card
    D. time may be saved by such action

2. Assume that you are the receptionist for Mr. Brown, an official in your department. It is your duty to permit only persons having important business to see this official; otherwise, you are to refer them to other members of the staff. A man tells you that he must see Mr. Brown on a very urgent and confidential matter. He gives you his name and says that Mr. Brown knows him, but he does not wish to tell you the nature of the matter.
   Of the following, the BEST action for you to take under these circumstances is to

    2.____

    A. permit this man to see Mr. Brown without further question since the matter seems to be urgent
    B. refer this man to another member of the staff, since Mr. Brown may not wish to see him
    C. call Mr. Brown and explain the situation to him, and ask him whether he wishes to see this man
    D. tell this man that you will permit him to see Mr. Brown only if he informs you of the nature of his business

3. You are given copies of an important official notice, together with a memorandum stating that each of the employees listed on the memorandum is to receive a copy of the official notice.
   In order to have definite proof that each of the employees listed has received a copy of the notice, the BEST of the following courses of action for you to take as you hand the notice to each of the employees is to

    3.____

    A. put your initial next to the employee's name on the memorandum
    B. ask the employee to sign the notice you have given in your presence
    C. have the employee put his signature next to his name on the memorandum
    D. ask the employee to read the notice in your presence

4. Suppose that you are assigned to the information window of a city department where you   4.___
come in daily contact with many people. On one occasion, a man asks you for some
information in a very arrogant and rude manner.
Of the following, the BEST reason for you to give this man the requested information
politely is that

   A. he may not mean to be rude; it may just be his manner of speech
   B. it is the duty of city employees to teach members of the public to be polite
   C. he will probably apologize for his manner when he sees that you are polite
   D. city employees are expected to be courteous to the public

5. Assume that you have been placed in charge of a stock room in a city department and   5.___
that one of your duties is to take a periodic inventory of the supplies you have on hand.
Of the following, the BEST justification for this procedure is

   A. you will know which supplies are running low
   B. accurate records need not be kept in all stock rooms
   C. you will become more familiar with the location of the different items in the stock
      room
   D. it will prevent the needless waste of supplies by the employees of the department

6. It is an accepted practice to have the initials of the person who dictates a letter, as well as   6.___
those of the person who types it, appear in the lower left-hand corner of the letter.
Of the following, the CHIEF justification for this procedure is that it

   A. may be used as a means of measuring output of work
   B. fixes responsibility
   C. aids in filing
   D. avoids the need for making carbon copies

7. Suppose that you are given several sheets containing an unalphabetized list of 500   7.___
names and a corresponding set of 500 disarranged cards. Your supervisor asks you to
check to see that for every name on the list there is a corresponding card.
Of the following, the MOST efficient procedure for you to follow is to

   A. arrange both the cards and the names on the list in alphabetical order and check
      one against the other
   B. alphabetize the list only and check each card in turn against the names on the list
   C. alphabetize the cards only and check each name on the list in turn against the
      cards
   D. alphabetize neither the cards nor the list, but take each card in turn and find the
      corresponding name on the list

8. The clerk could not recall the name of the person to whom his supervisor had requested   8.___
him to make a check payable. He therefore made it payable to *Cash.*
This action on the part of the clerk is

   A. to be praised; he showed ingenuity
   B. to be criticized; if lost, the check might be cashed by anyone finding it
   C. inexcusable; a check must be made payable to a definite person
   D. correct; in the future, he should make all checks payable to *Cash*

9. Assume that one of your duties as a clerk is to keep a constantly changing mailing list up-to-date.
Of the following, the BEST method for you to follow is to use use a(n)

    A. alphabetical card index with loose cards, one for each name
    B. bound volume with a separate page or group of pages for each letter
    C. loose-leaf notebook with names beginning with the same letter listed on the same sheet or group of sheets
    D. typed list, add names at end of the list, and retype periodically in proper alphabetical order

9.____

10. In evaluating the effectiveness of a filing system, the one of the following criteria which you should consider MOST important is the

    A. safety of material in the event of a fire
    B. ease with which material may be located
    C. quantity of papers which can be filed
    D. extent to which material in the filing system is being used

10.____

11. A set of cards numbered from 1 to 300 has been filed in numerical order in such a way that the highest number is at the front of the file and the lowest number is at the rear. It is desired that the cards be reversed to run in ascending order.
The BEST of the following methods that can be used in performing this task is to begin at the

    A. front of the file and remove the cards one at a time, placing each one face up on top of the one removed before
    B. front of the file and remove the cards one at a time, placing each one face down on top of the one removed before
    C. back of the file and remove the cards in small groups, placing each group face down on top of the group removed before
    D. back of the file and remove the cards one at a time, placing each one face up on top of the one removed before

11.____

12. A person would MOST likely make a *person-to-person* long distance telephone call when

    A. he does not know whether the person to whom he wishes to speak is in
    B. he wishes to speak to any person answering the telephone
    C. he knows that the person to whom he wishes to speak will answer the telephone
    D. the call is made before 7 P.M.

12.____

13. In a certain file room, it is customary, when removing a record from the files, to insert an *out* card in its place. A clerk suggests keeping, in addition, a chronological list of all records removed and the names of the employees who have removed them.
This suggestion would be of GREATEST value

    A. in avoiding duplication of work
    B. in enabling an employee to refile records more easily
    C. where records are frequently misfiled
    D. where records are frequently kept out longer than necessary

13.____

14. You are given a large batch of correspondence and asked to obtain the folder on file for   14.___
    each of the senders of these letters. The folders in your file room are kept in numerical
    order and an alphabetic cross-index file is maintained.
    Of the following, the BEST procedure would be for you to

    A. look up the numbers in the alphabetic file, then alphabetize the correspondence
       according to the senders' names and obtain the folders from the numerical file
    B. alphabetize the correspondence according to the senders' names, get the file num-
       bers from the alphabetic file, and obtain the folders from the numerical file
    C. alphabetize the correspondence and then look through the numerical file for the
       proper folders in the order in which your correspondence is arranged
    D. look through the numerical file, pulling out the folders as you come across them

15. Designing forms of the proper size is of the utmost importance. Certain sizes are best   15.___
    because they can be cut without waste from standard sheets of paper on which forms
    are printed and because they fit standard files and binders.
    The one of the following which is the MOST valid implication of the above passage is
    that

    A. the size of a form should be decided upon before the information is printed on it
    B. the size of a form should be such that it can be printed on paper without cutting
    C. the person designing a form should be acquainted with standard sizes in file cabi-
       nets and paper
    D. the purpose of a form is an important factor in the determination of its size

16. When an employee is encouraged by his supervisor to think of new ideas in connection   16.___
    with his work, the habit of improving work methods is fostered.
    The one of the following which is the MOST valid implication of the above statement is
    that

    A. the improvement of work methods should be the concern not only of the supervisor
       but of the employee as well
    B. an employee without initiative cannot perform his job well
    C. an employee may waste too much time in experimenting with new work methods
    D. an improved method for performing a task should not be used without the approval
       of the supervisor

17. The report on the work of the three employees furnishes definite proof that Jones is more   17.___
    efficient than Smith, and that Brown is less efficient than Jones.
    On the basis of the above information, the MOST accurate of the following statements
    is that

    A. Brown is more efficient than Smith
    B. Smith is more efficient than Brown
    C. Smith is not necessarily less efficient than Jones
    D. Brown is not necessarily more efficient than Smith

18. Almost all students with a high school average of 80% or over were admitted to the col-   18.___
    lege.
    On the basis of this statement, it would be MOST accurate to assume that

A. a high school average of 80% or over was required for admittance to the college
B. some students with a high school average of less than 80% were admitted to the college
C. a high school average of at least 80% was desirable but not necessary for admission to the college
D. some students with a high school average of at least 80% were not admitted to the college

Questions 19-21.

DIRECTIONS: Questions 19 to 21 are to be answered SOLELY on the basis of the information contained in the following passage.

It is common knowledge that ability to do a particular job and performance on the job do not always go hand-in-hand. Persons with great potential abilities sometimes fall down on the job because of laziness or lack of interest in the job, while persons with mediocre talents have often achieved excellent results through their industry and their loyalty to the interests of their employers. It is clear, therefore, that in a balanced personnel program, measures of employee ability need to be supplemented by measures of employee performance, for the final test of any employee is his performance on the job.

19. The MOST accurate of the following statements, on the basis of the above paragraph, is that   19._____

A. employees who lack ability are usually not industrious
B. an employee's attitudes are more important than his abilities
C. mediocre employees who are interested in their work are preferable to employees who possess great ability
D. superior capacity for performance should be supplemented with proper attitudes

20. On the basis of the above paragraph, the employee of most value to his employer is NOT necessarily the one who   20._____

A. best understands the significance of his duties
B. achieves excellent results
C. possesses the greatest talents
D. produces the greatest amount of work

21. According to the above paragraph, an employee's efficiency is BEST determined by an   21._____

A. appraisal of his interest in his work
B. evaluation of the work performed by him
C. appraisal of his loyalty to his employer
D. evaluation of his potential ability to perform his work

22. Assume that you know the capacity of a filing cabinet, the extent of which it is filled, and the daily rate at which material is being added to the file.
In order to estimate how many more days it will take for the cabinet to be filled to capacity, you should   22._____

A. divide the extent to which the cabinet is filled by the daily rate
B. take the difference between the capacity of the cabinet and the material in it, and multiply the result by the daily rate of adding material

C. divide the daily rate of adding material by the difference between the capacity of the cabinet and the material in it

D. take the difference between the capacity of the cabinet and the material in it, and divide the result by the daily rate of adding material

23. Suppose you have been asked to compute the average salary earned in your department during the past year. For each of the divisions of the department, you are given the number of employees and the average salary.
In order to find the requested overall average salary for the department, you should

    A. add the average salaries of the various divisions and divide the total by the number of divisions

    B. multiply the number of employees in each division by the corresponding average salary, add the results and divide the total by the number of employees in the department

    C. add the average salaries of the various divisions and divide the total by the total number of employees in the department

    D. multiply the sum of the average salaries of the various divisions by the total number of divisions and divide the resulting product by the total number of employees in the department

24. Three divisions within a department are working to complete a major six-month project with varying levels of responsibility. A manager asks you to prepare a chart or graph that indicates each division's share (by percentage) of the project's total expenses to date for review by a department supervisor. The most effective type of chart or graph to use in this case would be a

    A. pie chart   B. line graph
    C. bar graph   D. Venn diagram

25. A study of the grades of students in a certain college revealed that in 2005, 15% fewer students received a passing grade in mathematics than in 2004, whereas in 2006, the number of students passing mathematics increased 15% over 2005.
On the basis of this study, it would be MOST accurate to conclude that

    A. the same percentage of students passed mathematics in 2004 as in 2006

    B. of the three years studied, the greatest percentage of students passed mathematics in 2006

    C. the percentage of students who passed mathematics in 2006 was less than the percentage passing this subject in 2004

    D. the percentage of students passing mathematics in 2004 was 15% greater than the percentage of students passing this subject in 2006

26. Some authority must determine finally whether constitutional guarantees mean literally and absolutely what they say, or something less or perchance more.
In the American system of government, that authority rests with the

    A. elected representatives in Congress
    B. executive branch of the federal government
    C. courts
    D. state legislatures

27. Almost all city departments obtain their supplies and equipment through the Department of Purchase.
Of the following, the CHIEF justification for this procedure is to effect savings by means of

    A. large-scale consumption of standard office supplies
    B. competitive bidding
    C. centralized buying
    D. non-profit purchasing

27.____

28. The one of the following federal agencies which is MOST concerned with the conservation of natural resources in this country is the

    A. Department of Interior
    B. Federal Trade Commission
    C. Department of Commerce
    D. Department of State

28.____

29. A city employee who is familiar with economic affairs should know that a period of inflation can BEST be characterized as a period when

    A. there is universal prosperity
    B. savings can buy fewer things than anticipated
    C. the cost of necessities is high and the cost of luxuries is low
    D. the value of money is increased

29.____

30. A clerk interested in world affairs should know that UNESCO is concerned MAINLY with international cooperation

    A. in the control of atomic power
    B. in the relocation of refugees
    C. to raise health standards throughout the world
    D. through the free exchange of information on education, art, and science

30.____

31. Suppose that your supervisor gives you a folder of approximately 200 letters, arranged chronologically, and a list of the names of the writers of these letters, arranged alphabetically. He asks you to verify, without disarranging the order of the letters, that there is a letter in the folder for each name on the list. Of the following, the BEST procedure for you to follow is to

    A. glance at each of the letters in the folder in turn and place a light pencil check on the alphabetical list next to the name of the person writing that letter
    B. glance at each of the letters in the folder in turn and place a light pencil check on each letter if there is a corresponding name on the alphabetical list
    C. rearrange the letters in alphabetical order and verify that there is a one-to-one relationship between letters and names
    D. rewrite the names on the list in chronological order and verify that there is a one-to-one relationship between letters and names

31.____

32. Suppose that you will not be able to complete today an important job that you have been assigned and that you expect to be out of the office the next few days.
In general, the BEST action for you to take before leaving the office at the end of the day is to

    A. apportion the remainder of your work equally among the other clerks in your office
    B. arrange your work neatly on top of your desk

32.____

C.   tell your supervisor exactly how much of the work you have been able to do
D.   lock your work in your desk so that your work cannot be disturbed in your absence

33.   Suppose that your supervisor has asked you to make a copy of a statistical table.   33.___
In general, the BEST method for checking the copy you prepare in order to make certain that the copy is absolutely accurate is for you to

A.   make a second copy of the table and compare the two copies
B.   have another clerk read the original table aloud to you while you read the copy
C.   compare all totals in the two tables, for if the totals check, the copy is probably accurate
D.   check the one or two points in the table at which an error is most likely to be made

34.   Suppose that, in the course of your work, you frequently come into contact with the public.   34.___
The one of the following which is the BEST reason for courtesy in all your contacts with the public is that

A.   most individuals are fully aware of the methods and procedures of city departments
B.   some individuals who come to city agencies for information or assistance are so domineering in their attitude that it is difficult to be polite
C.   no employee of a private business organization would dare to be discourteous to a customer
D.   a favorable attitude on the part of the public toward civil service employees is necessary for maintenance of the merit system

35.   *It is good office practice, when answering the telephone, to give immediately the name of*   35.___
the office in which you work.
Of the following, the BEST reason for following this practice is that it

A.   identifies immediately the particular person answering the telephone
B.   avoids loss of time due to mistaken or uncertain identity
C.   stimulates employees to answer the telephone quickly
D.   indicates directly that your supervisor is not in the office

Questions 36-44.

DIRECTIONS: Questions 36 to 44 consist of 9 groups of names. Consider each group of names as a unit. Determine in what position the name printed in ITALICS would be if the names in the group were CORRECTLY arranged in alphabetical order. If the name in italics should be first, print the letter A; if second, print the letter B; if third, print the letter C; if fourth, print the letter D; and if fifth, print the letter E. Indicate the answer in the space at the right. Below are some rules for alphabetizing which you are to use as a guide in answering these items:

1.   Arrange alphabetically, first, according to surnames; when surnames are the same, then according to given names or initials; when given names or initials are also the same, then according to middle names or initials.
2.   An initial precedes a name beginning with the same letter. For example: J. Martin precedes James Martin.

3. A name without a middle name or initial precedes the same name having a middle name or initial.
   For example: James Martin precedes James E. Martin.
4. Treat all abbreviations as if spelled out in full when the names for which they stand are commonly understood.
5. Arrange names beginning with "Mc" or "Mac" in their exact alphabetic order as spelled.
6. Treat names containing numerals as if numerals were spelled out.
7. The names of business organizations which do not include the name of a person are alphabetized as written, subject to the provisions of Rule 8.
8. Disregard the following in alphabetizing: the, and, titles and designations as Dr., Mr., Mrs., Jr., and Sr.

SAMPLE ITEM:

J.W. Martin	(2)
James E. Martin	(4)
J. Martin	(1)
George Martins	(5)
James Martin	(3)

The correct alphabetic order is indicated alongside the names in the sample item, and the correct answer should be D.

36. Albert Brown   36._____
    James Borenstein
    Frieda Albrecht
    Samuel Brown
    George Appelman

37. James Ryn   37._____
    Francis Ryan
    Wm. Roanan
    Frances S. Ryan
    Francis P. Ryan

38. Norman Fitzgibbons   38._____
    Charles F. Franklin
    Jas. Fitzgerald
    Andrew Fitzsimmons
    James P. Fitzgerald

39. Hugh F. Martenson   39._____
    A.S. Martinson
    Albert Martinsen
    Albert S. Martinson
    M. Martanson

40. Aaron M. Michelson   40._____
    Samuel Michels
    Arthur L. Michaelson, Sr.
    John Michell
    Daniel Michelsohn

41. *Chas. R. Connolly*
    Frank Conlon
    Charles S. Connolly
    Abraham Cohen
    Chas. Conolly

41.___

42. James McCormack
    Ruth MacNamara
    Kathryn McGillicuddy
    Frances Mason
    Arthur MacAdams

42.___

43. Dr. Francis Karell
    John Joseph Karelsen, jr.
    John J. Karelsen, Sr.
    Mrs. Jeanette Kelly
    Estelle Karel

43.___

44. *The 5th Ave. Bus Co.*
    The Baltimore and Ohio Railroad
    3rd Ave. Elevated Co.
    The 4th Ave. Trolley Line

44.___

Questions 45-53.

DIRECTIONS: The following table contains certain information about employees in a city bureau. Questions 45 to 53 are to be answered on the basis of the facts given in this table.

RECORD OF EMPLOYEES IN A CITY BUREAU

NAME	TITLE	AGE	ANNUAL SALARY	YEARS OF SERVICE	EXAMINATION RATING
Jones	Clerk	34	$20,400	10	82
Smith	Stenographer	25	19,200	2	72
Black	Typist	19	14,400	1	71
Brown	Stenographer	36	25,200	12	88
Thomas	Accountant	49	41,200	21	91
Gordon	Clerk	31	30,000	8	81
Johnson	Stenographer	26	26,400	5	75
White	Accountant	53	36,000	30	90
Spencer	Clerk	42	27,600	19	85
Taylor	Typist	24	21,600	5	74
Simpson	Accountant	37	50,000	11	87
Reid	Typist	20	12,000	2	72
Fulton	Accountant	55	55,000	31	100
Chambers	Clerk	22	15,600	4	75
Calhoun	Stenographer	48	28,800	16	80

45. The name of the employee whose salary would be the middle one if all the salaries were ranked in order of magnitude is

   A. White   B. Johnson   C. Brown   D. Spencer

45.____

46. The combined monthly salary of all the stenographers exceeds the combined monthly salary of all the clerks by

   A. $6,000   B. $500   C. $22,800   D. $600

46.____

47. The age of the employee who received the HIGHEST rating in the examination among those who have less than 10 years of service is _____ years.

   A. 22   B. 31   C. 55   D. 34

47.____

48. The average examination rating of those employees who had 15 years of service or more as compared with the average examination rating of those employees who had 5 years of service or less is MOST NEARLY

   A. 16 points greater   B. 7 points greater
   C. 10 points less   D. 25 points greater

48.____

49. The name of the youngest employee whose monthly salary is more than $1,000 per month and who has more than one year of service is

   A. Reid   B. Black   C. Chambers   D. Taylor

49.____

50. The name of the employee who received an examination rating of over 85%, who has more than 15 years of service, and who earns a yearly salary of more than $25,000 but less than $40,000 is

   A. Thomas   B. Spencer   C. Calhoun   D. White

50.____

KEY (CORRECT ANSWERS)

1.	D	11.	A	21.	B	31.	A	41.	C
2.	C	12.	A	22.	D	32.	C	42.	C
3.	C	13.	D	23.	B	33.	B	43.	D
4.	D	14.	B	24.	A	34.	D	44.	B
5.	A	15.	C	25.	A	35.	B	45.	B
6.	B	16.	A	26.	C	36.	E	46.	B
7.	C	17.	D	27.	C	37.	D	47.	B
8.	B	18.	D	28.	A	38.	A	48.	A
9.	A	19.	D	29.	B	39.	E	49.	C
10.	B	20.	C	30.	D	40.	D	50.	D

TEST 2

DIRECTIONS: Each question or incomplete statement is followed by several suggested answers or completions. Select the one that BEST answers the question or completes the statement. *PRINT THE LETTER OF THE CORRECT ANSWER IN THE SPACE AT THE RIGHT.*

1. The annual salary of the HIGHEST paid stenographer is

    A. more than twice as great as the salary of the youngest employee
    B. greater than the salary of the oldest typist but not as great as the salary of the oldest clerk
    C. greater than the salary of the highest paid typist but not as great as the salary of the lowest paid accountant
    D. less than the combined salaries of the two youngest typists

    1.___

2. The number of employees whose annual salary is more than $15,600 but less than $28,800 and who have at least 5 years of service is

    A. 11   B. 8   C. 6   D. 5

    2.___

3. Of the following, it would be MOST accurate to state that the

    A. youngest employee is lowest with respect to number of years of service, examination rating, and salary
    B. oldest employee is highest with respect to number of years of service, examination rating, but not with respect to salary
    C. annual salary of the youngest clerk is $1,200 more than the annual salary of the youngest typist and $2,400 less than the annual salary of the youngest stenographer
    D. difference in age between the youngest and oldest typist is less than one-fourth the difference in age between the youngest and oldest stenographer

    3.___

4. *He advocated a new course of action.* The word *advocated* means MOST NEARLY

    A. described   B. refused to discuss
    C. argued against   D. supported

    4.___

5. A clerk who is assigned to make a *facsimile* of a report should make a copy which is

    A. exact   B. larger   C. smaller   D. edited

    5.___

6. *A city employee must be a person of integrity.* The word *integrity* means MOST NEARLY

    A. intelligence   B. competence
    C. honesty   D. keenness

    6.___

7. A person who displays *apathy* is

    A. irritated   B. confused
    C. indifferent   D. insubordinate

    7.___

8. *The supervisor admonished the clerk for his tardiness.* The word *admonished* means MOST NEARLY

    A. reproved   B. excused   C. transferred   D. punished

    8.___

9. A *lucrative* business is one which is   9.____

    A. unprofitable   B. gainful   C. unlawful   D. speculative

10. To say that the work is *tedious* means MOST NEARLY that it is   10.____

    A. technical   B. interesting
    C. tiresome   D. confidential

11. A *vivacious* person is one who is   11.____

    A. kind   B. talkative   C. lively   D. well-dressed

12. An *innocuous* statement is one which is   12.____

    A. forceful   B. harmless   C. offensive   D. brief

13. To say that the order was *rescinded* means MOST NEARLY that it was   13.____

    A. revised   B. canceled
    C. misinterpreted   D. confirmed

14. To say that the administrator *amplified* his remarks means MOST NEARLY that the   14.____
remarks were

    A. shouted   B. expanded
    C. carefully analyzed   D. summarized briefly

15. *Peremptory commands will be resented in any office.* The word *peremptory* means   15.____
MOST NEARLY

    A. unexpected   B. unreasonable
    C. military   D. dictatorial

16. A clerk should know that the word *sporadic* means MOST NEARLY   16.____

    A. occurring regularly   B. sudden
    C. scattered   D. disturbing

17. To *vacillate* means MOST NEARLY to   17.____

    A. lubricate   B. waver   C. decide   D. investigate

18. A *homogeneous* group of persons is characterized by its   18.____

    A. similarity   B. teamwork
    C. discontent   D. differences

19. A *vindictive* person is one who is   19.____

    A. prejudiced   B. unpopular   C. petty   D. revengeful

20. The abbreviation *e.g.* occurs frequently in written matter and is commonly taken to mean   20.____

    A. note carefully   B. for example
    C. entire group   D. and others

21. The abbreviation *i.e.* also occurs frequently in written matter and is commonly taken to   21.____
mean

    A. that is   B. the same
    C. in the same place   D. and others

Questions 22-37.

DIRECTIONS: Each of the sentences numbered 22 to 37 may be classified MOST appropriately under one of the following four categories:
- A. faulty because of incorrect grammar
- B. faulty because of incorrect punctuation
- C. faulty because of incorrect capitalization
- D. correct

Examine each sentence carefully. Then, in the correspondingly numbered space at the right, print the letter preceding the option which is the BEST of the four suggested above. All incorrect sentences contain but one type of error. Consider a sentence correct if it contains none of the types of errors mentioned, even though there may be other correct ways of expressing the same thought.

22.   The desk, as well as the chairs, were moved out of the office.   22.___

23.   The clerk whose production was greatest for the month won a day's vacation as first prize.   23.___

24.   Upon entering the room, the employees were found hard at work at their desks.   24.___

25.   John Smith our new employee always arrives at work on time.   25.___

26.   Punish whoever is guilty of stealing the money.   26.___

27.   Intelligent and persistent effort lead to success no matter what the job may be.   27.___

28.   The secretary asked, "can you call again at three o'clock?"   28.___

29.   He told us, that if the report was not accepted at the next meeting, it would have to be rewritten.   29.___

30.   He would not have sent the letter if he had known that it would cause so much excitement.   30.___

31.   We all looked forward to him coming to visit us.   31.___

32.   If you find that you are unable to complete the assignment please notify me as soon as possible.   32.___

33.   Every girl in the office went home on time but me; there was still some work for me to finish.   33.___

34.   He wanted to know who the letter was addressed to, Mr. Brown or Mr. Smith.   34.___

35.   "Mr. Jones, he said, please answer this letter as soon as possible."   35.___

36.   The new clerk had an unusual accent inasmuch as he was born and educated in the south.   36.___

37.   Although he is younger than her, he earns a higher salary.   37.___

Questions 38-45.

DIRECTIONS: Questions 38 to 45 consist of four words each. In each item, one of the words may be spelled incorrectly or all the words may be spelled correctly. If one of the words in an item is spelled incorrectly, print in the correspondingly numbered space at the right the letter preceding the word which is spelled incorrectly. If all four words are spelled correctly, print the letter E.

38.	A. temporary	B. existance	C. complimentary	D. altogether	38.____
39.	A. privilege	B. changeable	C. jeopardize	D. commitment	39.____
40.	A. grievous	B. alloted	C. outrageous	D. mortgage	40.____

41.   A. tempermental   B. bookkeeping   41.____
        B. accommodating   D. panicky

42.	A. auxiliary	B. indispensable	C. ecstasy	D. fiery	42.____
43.	A. dissapear	B. buoyant	C. imminent	D. parallel	43.____
44.	A. loosly	B. medicine	C. schedule	D. defendant	44.____
45.	A. endeavor	B. persuade	C. retroactive	D. desparate	45.____

Questions 46-50

DIRECTIONS: Each of Questions 46 to 50 contains five words in italics, one of which is not in keeping with the meaning which the question is evidently intended to carry. The five words in italics in each item are reprinted after the question. On the correspondingly numbered space at the right, print the letter preceding the one of the five words which does MOST to spoil the true meaning of the question.

46. City departments having direct *contact* with the *public* should be located *if* they are 46.____
readily *accessible* to those *coming* to the office on business.

     A. contact   B. public   C. if
     D. accessible   E. coming

47. Many communications covering a *specific* subject can be form letters, but going to 47.____
extremes in this matter should be guarded against; to send a form letter when a specially
composed letter should be used is *often* the most mistaken *extravagance*.

     A. specific   B. extremes   C. composed
     D. often   E. extravagance

48. In order to prevent *unavoidable* accidents, a *safety* engineer designs and superintends 48.____
the *installation* of safety devices. If employees always used the safety devices *provided,*
there would be *few* accidents.

     A. unavoidable   B. safety   C. installation
     D. provided   E. few

49. Most business records have an intangible *value* to the business which *can* be measured in dollars and cents. They are the *result* of figures and facts obtained from many sources and are often *impossible* to replace at *any* cost of time or money.

    A. value   B. can   C. result   D. impossible E. any

49.___

50. A major advantage gained by a company that uses only one *particular* type of a machine is greater *efficiency* of operation. If, for example, all the calculating machines in an office are identical, it is *trifling* that time is *saved* by employees in *learning* how to operate these machines.

    A. particular   B. efficiency   C. trifling
    D. saved   E. learning

50.___

KEY (CORRECT ANSWERS)

1. C	11. C	21. A	31. A	41. A
2. D	12. B	22. A	32. B	42. E
3. D	13. B	23. D	33. D	43. A
4. D	14. B	24. A	34. A	44. A
5. A	15. D	25. B	35. B	45. D
6. C	16. C	26. D	36. C	46. C
7. C	17. B	27. A	37. A	47. E
8. A	18. A	28. C	38. B	48. A
9. B	19. D	29. A	39. E	49. B
10. C	20. B	30. D	40. B	50. C

EXAMINATION SECTION
TEST 1

DIRECTIONS: Each question or incomplete statement is followed by several suggested answers or completions. Select the one that BEST answers the question or completes the statement. *PRINT THE LETTER OF THE CORRECT ANSWER IN THE SPACE AT THE RIGHT.*

1. Assume that you are one of several clerks employed in the office of a city department.   1._____
   Members of the public occasionally visit the office to obtain information. Because your desk
   is nearest the entrance to the office, most of these visitors direct their inquiries to you. One
   morning when every one including yourself is busy, a visitor enters the office and asks you
   for some readily available information.
   Of the following, the BEST action for you to take is to

   A. disregard his question in the hope that he will direct his inquiry to another clerk
   B. inform him politely that you are busy now and ask him to return in the afternoon
   C. give him the requested information concisely but courteously and then continue
      with your work
   D. advise him to write a letter to your department so that the information can be sent
      to him

2. As a clerk in the payroll bureau of a city department, you have been assigned the task of   2._____
   checking several payroll sheets. Your supervisor has informed you that these payroll sheets
   are needed by another department and must be sent to that department by 4 P.M. that day.
   After you have worked for a few hours, you realize that you will be unable to complete this
   assignment on time.
   Of the following, the BEST action for you to take first is to

   A. ask a co-worker to help you
   B. check only those payroll sheets which you think are most important
   C. make sure that the payroll sheets which have been checked are sent out on time
   D. inform your supervisor of the situation

3. The switchboard operator of Department X refers a call to the department's Personnel   3._____
   Bureau. Miss Jones, a clerk in the Personnel Bureau, answers this call.
   Of the following ways of answering this call, the MOST acceptable one is for
   Miss Jones to say

   A. "Hello."
   B. "Personnel Bureau, Miss Jones speaking."
   C. "Miss Jones speaking. To whom do you wish to speak?!'
   D. "Hello. This is Miss Jones of Department X."

4. A clerk in the mailing division of a large city department should be acquainted with the   4._____
   functions of the other divisions of the department CHIEFLY because he will be

   A. able to answer questions asked by visitors regarding the department
   B. more conscientious in doing his work if he knows that other divisions of the
      department perform important functions
   C. in a better position to make suggestions for improving the work of the various
      divisions of the department
   D. able to determine the proper division to which mail is to be forwarded

5. The central filing unit of a certain city department keeps in its files records used by the various bureaus in connection with their daily work.
   It is desirable for the clerks in this filing unit to refile records as soon as possible after they have been returned by the different bureaus CHIEFLY because

    5.___

    A. records which are needed can be located most easily if they have been filed
    B. such procedure develops commendable work habits among the employees
    C. records which are not filed immediately are usually filed incorrectly
    D. the accumulation of records to be filed gives the office a disorderly appearance

6. The active and inactive file material of an office is to be filed in several four-drawer filing cabinets.
   Of the following, the BEST method of filing the material is, in general, to

    6.___

    A. keep inactive material in the upper drawers of the file cabinet so that such material may be easily removed for disposal
    B. keep active material in the upper drawers so that the amount of stooping by clerks using the files is reduced to a minimum
    C. assign drawers in the file cabinets alternately to active and to inactive material so that file material can be transferred easily from the active to the inactive files
    D. assign file cabinets alternately to active and to inactive material so that cross-references between the two types of material can be easily made

7. Of the following, the BEST reason for using form letters is that they

    7.___

    A. enable an individual to transmit unpleasant or disappointing communications in a gentle and sympathetic manner
    B. present the facts in a terse, business-like manner
    C. save the time of both the dictator and the typist in answering letters dealing with similar matters
    D. are flexible and can be easily changed to meet varying needs and complex situations

8. City agencies use either window envelopes or plain envelopes in mailing their correspondence, depending upon the type of mail being sent out.
   When a mail clerk uses a window envelope rather than a plain envelope, he should be especially careful in

    8.___

    A. sealing and stamping the envelope
    B. affixing the correct amount of postage
    C. folding and inserting the communication
    D. checking the return address

9. As a mail clerk, you have been instructed to make sure that an important letter is received by the person to whom it is addressed.

    9.___

    Of the following, the BEST action for you to take is to send the letter by
    A. registered mail   B. special delivery
    C. air mail   D. first-class mail

10. In filing, a clerk must often attach several papers together before placing them in the files.   10._____
Usually, the MOST desirable of the following methods of attaching these papers is to

    A. pin them together
    B. staple them together
    C. attach them with a paper clip
    D. glue them together

11. It is a common practice in answering a letter of inquiry to make a copy of the reply.   11._____
A clerk should know that, of the following, the BEST procedure to follow with the copy
is to

    A. file it with the letter it answers
    B. file it alphabetically in a separate copy file
    C. file it chronologically in a separate copy file and destroy the copy after thirty days
    D. enclose it with the letter of reply

12. Suppose that much of the work of your office involves computation of statistical data.   12._____
This computation is being done without the use of adding machines. You believe the
work could be done more efficiently if adding machines were used.
Of the following, the BEST action for you to take is to

    A. carry out your assignments without comment, since it is not your function to
       recommend revisions in office practices
    B. have other clerks who agree with you sign a memorandum requesting your
       supervisor to install adding machines
    C. obtain concrete facts to support your views and then take this matter up with
       your supervisor
    D. point out to your supervisor every time an error is made that it would not have
       occurred if adding machines had been used

13. A clerk employed in the central file section of a city department has been requested to   13._____
obtain a certain card which is kept in an alphabetic file containing several thousand cards.
The clerk finds that this card is not in its proper place and that there is no out card to aid
him in tracing its location.
Of the following, the course of action which would be LEAST helpful to him in locating the
missing card would be for him to

    A. secure the assistance of his superior
    B. look at several cards filed immediately before and after the place where the
       missing card should be filed
    C. ask the other clerks in the file section whether they have this card
    D. prepare an out card and place it where the missing card should be filed

14. The one of the following types of computer software which requires the use of   14._____
spreadsheets is

    A. Excel   B. Acrobat   C. Outlook   D. Safari

15. A clerk assigned to file correspondence in a subject file would be MOST concerned with   15._____
the
    A. name of the sender   B. main topic of the correspondence
    C. city and state of the sender   D. date of the correspondence

16. Assume that you are responsible for storing and distributing supplies in a city department. 16.___
The one of the following factors which you should consider LEAST important in selecting a suitable place in the stock room for storing a particular item is

    A. the frequency of requests for it
    B. its perishability
    C. its size
    D. the importance of the bureaus using it

17. A clerk in charge of the supply room of a city department notices that one of the bureaus 17.___
is asking for considerably more stationery than it has requested in the past.
For him to inquire into the reasons for the increased demand would be

    A. *desirable*; the amount of stationery used by a bureau should remain constant
    B. *undesirable*; the increased demand may be due to waste, a condition beyond his control
    C. *desirable*; he will be better able to estimate future needs for stationery
    D. *undesirable*; he may be accused of meddling in matters which do not concern him

18. One of the first things an executive usually looks for when he arrives in the morning is 18.___
his mail.
Of the following, the MOST valid implication on the basis of this statement is that

    A. letters addressed to an executive should be answered in the order in which they are received
    B. whenever possible, mail for an executive should be on his desk before his arrival in the morning
    C. letters to a city department should be addressed to the department head
    D. the first task of an executive upon his arrival in the morning should be to answer his mail

19. Persons in the employ of a public agency generally come into contact with many people 19.___
outside of working hours. In these contacts, the government employee represents to the public the quality, competence, and stature of public employees as a group.
The one of the following statements which is the MOST valid implication of the above observation is that

    A. the responsibilities of a public employee cease after office hours
    B. government employees who come into contact with the public during working hours should be more efficient than those who have no contact with the public
    C. a public employee, by his behavior during social activities, can raise the prestige of public employment
    D. employees of a private company have greater responsibilities during office hours than employees of a public agency

20. Filing, in a way, is a form of recording. 20.___

The one of the following which BEST explains this statement is that
    A. no other records are required if a proper filing system is used
    B. important records should, as a rule, be kept in filing cabinets
    C. a good system of record keeping eliminates the necessity for a filing system
    D. filing a letter or document is, in effect, equivalent to making a record of its contents

21. In standardizing clerical tasks, one should attempt to eliminate the undesirable elements   21._____
    and to retain the desirable ones.
    Of the following, the MOST valid implication of the above statement is that

    A. a task containing undesirable elements cannot be standardized
    B. standardized clerical tasks should not contain any unnecessary steps
    C. interesting clerical tasks are easier to standardize than monotonous clerical tasks
    D. a clerical task cannot have both desirable and undesirable elements

22. The efficiency of office workers in affected by the quality of the services provided to   22._____
    facilitate their work.
    The one of the following statements which is the BEST illustration of the above judgment
    is that

    A. a poorly run mail room will hamper the work of the office staff
    B. continual tardiness on the part of an office worker will be reflected in the
       erformance of his work
    C. a system of promoting office workers through competitive examinations will
       increase their efficiency
    D. the use of a time clock will improve the quality of the work performed

23. In elections held in various states, the provisions relating to veterans' preference have   23._____
    been amended to conform with Federal practice.
    In general, the MOST accurate statement regarding veterans' preference in civil service
    open competitive examinations for original appointment is that

    A. disabled veterans passing an examination will be given 10 additional points and
       non-disabled veterans passing an examination will be given 5 additional points
    B. disabled veterans passing an examination will be placed on top of the eligible list;
       non-disabled veterans will be placed after them; and non-veterans will be placed
       last on the list
    C. only disabled veterans will be given 5 additional points; no additional points will
       be given to nondisabled veterans
    D. the granting of additional points to all disabled and non-disabled veterans will be
       discontinued

24. Suppose that you are assigned to the information desk in your department. Your function   24._____
    is to give information to members of the public who telephone or call in person. It is a busy
    period of the year. There is a line of seventeen people waiting to speak to you. Because you
    are constantly being interrupted by telephone calls for information, however, you are unable
    to give any attention to the people waiting on line. The line is increasing in length.
    Of the following, the BEST action for you to take is to

    A. explain courteously to the people on line that you will probably be unable to help
       them
    B. advise the people at the end of the line that you will probably not reach them for
       some time and suggest that they come back when you are less busy
    C. ask the switchboard operator to answer telephone requests for information herself
       instead of putting the calls on your extension
    D. ask your supervisor to assign another clerk to answer telephone calls so that you
       can give your full attention to the people on line

25. Suppose that you are acting as the receptionist in your department. A man comes up to   25.___
you, introduces himself as Mr. Smith, and says that he has an appointment with Mr. Brown,
one of the clerks in your department. You know that Mr. Brown has been called out of the
office for a few days on important business. Upon learning of Mr. Brown's absence,
Mr. Smith asks whether someone else can help him. For you to telephone Mr. Brown's office
and ask whether some other clerk there can help Mr. Smith would be WISE mainly because

    A. Mr. Smith's business is probably confidential
    B. another clerk has probably been assigned to do Mr. Brown's work in Mr. Brown's
       absence
    C. Mr. Brown may return unexpectedly
    D. it is uncertain whether Mr. Smith actually does have an appointment with Mr. Brown

26. One of your duties may be to deliver copies of administrative orders to administrators   26.___
in your department. It is not necessary for an administrator to sign
a receipt for his copy of an order. One of the administrators to whom you are requested to
deliver a copy of an order is not at his desk when you make your usual tour of the office.
Of the following, the BEST action for you to take is to

    A. keep this order until a later order is issued and then deliver both orders at the same time
    B. wait until you meet the administrator in the corridor and give him his copy in person
    C. leave a note on the administrator's desk requesting him to call
    D. leave the administrator's copy of the order on his desk

27. One of your duties may be to deliver inter-office mail to all of the offices in the   27.___
department in which you work.
Of the following, the BEST procedure for you to follow before you deliver the letters is,
in general, to arrange them on the basis of the

    A. offices to which the letters are to be delivered
    B. dates on which the letters were written
    C. specific persons by whom the letters were signed
    D. offices from which the letters come

28. The population census of the country is undertaken every ten years by the United States   28.___
Department of
    A. Labor   B. the Treasury   C. Commerce   D. the Interior

29. Of the following pairs of offices in the Federal government, the pair which is held by the   29.___
same individual is
    A. Secretary of Defense and Secretary of the Army
    B. Chairman of the Atomic Energy Commission and Chairman of the Tennessee
       Valley Authority
    C. Chief Justice of the United States Supreme Court and Attorney General
    D. Vice President of the United States and President of the Senate

30. A clerk who is familiar with the organization and activities of the United Nations should   30.___
know, of the following statements, the MOST accurate one is that
    A. the permanent headquarters of the United Nations is in Geneva, Switzerland
    B. devaluation of the currency of a member nation must be approved by the
       United Nations General Assembly
    C. there are five permanent members on the United Nations Security Council
    D. the Economic Cooperation Administration (ECA) is under the jurisdiction of the
       United Nations Secretary General

7

31. In anticipation of a seasonal increase in the amount of work to be performed by his division, a division chief prepared the following list of additional temporary employees needed by his division and the amount of time they would be employed:
   26 cashiers, each at $24,000 a year, for 2 months
   15 laborers, each at $85.00 a day, for 50 days
   6 clerks, each at $21,000 a year, for 3 months
   The total approximate cost for this additional personnel would be MOST NEARLY

   A. $200,000   B. $250,000   C. $500,000   D. $600,000

31._____

32. A calculating machine company offered to sell a city agency 4 calculating machines at a discount of 15% from the list price, and to allow the agency $85 for each of its two old machines. The list price of the new machines is $625 per machine.
   If the city agency accepts this offer, the amount of money it will have to provide for the purchase of these four machines is

   A. $1,785   B. $2,295   C. $1,955   D. $1,836

32._____

33. A stationery buyer was offered bond paper at the following price scale:
   $2.86 per ream for the first 1,000 reams
   $2.60 per ream for the next 4,000 reams
   $2.40 per ream for each additional ream beyond 5,000 reams
   If the buyer ordered 10,000 reams of paper, the average cost per ream, computed to the NEAREST cent, was

   A. $2.48   B. $2.53   C. $2.62   D. $2.72

33._____

34. A clerk has 5.70% of his salary deducted for his retirement pension.
   If this clerk's annual salary is $20,400, the monthly deduction for his retirement pension is

   A. $298.20   B. $357.90   C. $1,162.80   D. $96.90

34._____

35. In a certain bureau, two-thirds of the employees are clerks and the remainder is typists.
   If there are 90 clerks, then the number of typists in this bureau is

   A. 135   B. 45   C. 120   D. 30

35._____

Questions 36-45.

DIRECTIONS: Assume that the code tables shown below are used by a city department in classifying its employees. Questions 36 to 45 are to be answered on the basis of these tables. In accordance with these code tables, each employee in the department is assigned a code number consisting of ten digits arranged from left to right in the following order:
   I.   Division in which Employed
   II.   Title of Position
   III. Annual Salary
   IV.   Age
   V.   Number of Years Employed in Department

   Example: A clerk is 21 years old, has been employed in the department for three years, and is working in the Supply Division at a yearly salary of $25,000. His code number should be 90-115-13-02-2.

8

Questions 36-45.

DIRECTIONS: Assume that the code tables shown below are used by a city department in classifying its employees. Questions 36 to 45 are to be answered on the basis of these tables. In accordance with these code tables, each employee in the department is assigned a code number consisting of ten digits arranged from left to right in the following order:

VI.   Division in which Employed
VII. Title of Position
VIII. Annual Salary
IX.   Age
X.   Number of Years Employed in Department

Example: A clerk is 21 years old, has been employed in the department for three years, and is working in the Supply Division at a yearly salary of $25,000. His code number should be 90-115-13-02-2.

DEPARTMENTAL CODE

TABLE I		TABLE II		TABLE III		TABLE IV		TABLE V	
Code No.	Division in Which Employed	Code No.	Title of position	Code No.	Annual Salary	Code No.	Age	Code No.	No. of years Employed in Dept.
10-	Accounting Division	115-	Clek	11-	$18,000 or less	01-	under 20 yrs	1-	less than 1 yrs
20-	Construction Division	155-	Typist	12-	$18,001 to $24,000	02-	20 to 29 yrs	2-	1 to 5 yrs
30-	Engineering Division	175-	Steno- grapher	13-	$24,001 to $30,000	03-	30 to 39 yrs	3-	6 to 10 yrs
40-	Information Division	237-	Book- Keeper	14-	$30,001 to $36,000	04-	40 to 49 yrs	4-	11 to 15 yrs
50-	Maintenance Division	345-	Statis- tician	15-	$36,001 to $45,000	05-	50 to 59 yrs	5-	16 to 25 yrs
60-	Personnel Division	545-	Store- Keeper	16-	$45,001 to $60,000	06-	62 to 69 yrs	6-	26 to 35 yrs
70-	Record Division	633-	Drafts- Man	17-	$60,001 to $70,000	07- over	70 yrs or over	7-	36 yrs. or over
80-	Research Division	665-	Civil- Engineer	18-	$70,001 or over				
90-	Supply Division	865-	Machinist						
		915-	Porter						

36. A draftsman employed in the Engineering Division yearly salary of $34,800 is 36 years old and has employed in the department for 9 years.
He should be coded

    A. 20-633-13-04-3   B. 50-665-14-04-4
    C. 30-865-13-03-4   D. 30-633-14-03-3

36._____

37. A porter employed in the Maintenance Division at a yearly salary of $28,800 is 52 years old and has been employed in the department for 6 years.
He should be coded

    A. 50-915-12-03-3   B. 90-545-12-05-3
    C. 50-915-13-05-3   D. 90-545-13-03-3

37._____

38. Richard White, who has been employed in the department for 12 years, receives $50,000 a year as a civil engineer in the Construction Division. He is 38 years old.
He should be coded
    A. 20-665-16-03-4   B. 20-665-15-02-1
    C. 20-633-14-04-2   D. 20-865-15-02-5

38._____

39. An 18-year-old clerk appointed to the department six months ago is assigned to the Record Division. His annual salary is $21,600.
He should be coded

    A. 70-115-11-01-1   B. 70-115-12-01-1
    C. 70-115-12-02-1   D. 70-155-12-01-1

39._____

40. An employee has been coded 40-155-12-03-3.
Of the following statements made regarding this employee, the MOST accurate one is that he is

    A. a clerk who has been employed in the department for at least 6 years
    B. a typist who receives an annual salary which does not exceed $24,000
    C. under 30 years of age and has been employed in the department for at least 11 years
    D. employed in the Supply Division at a salary which exceeds $18,000 per annum

40._____

41. Of the following statements regarding an employee who is coded 60-175-13-01-2, the LEAST accurate statement is that this employee
    A. is a stenographer in the Personnel Division
    B. has been employed in the department for at least one year
    C. receives an annual salary which exceeds $24,000
    D. is more than 20 years of age

41._____

42. The following are the names of our employees of the department with their code numbers:

James Black, 80-345-15-03-4;
William White, 30-633-14-03-4;
Sam Green, 80-115-12-02-3;
John Jones, 10-237-13-04-5.

42._____

If a salary increase is to be given to the employees who have been employed in the department for 11 years or more and who earn less than $36,001 a year, the two of the above employees who will receive a salary increase are

    A. John Jones and William White
    B. James Black and Sam Green
    C. James Black and William White
    D. John Jones and Sam Green

43. Code number 50-865-14-02-6, which has been assigned to a machinist, contains an   43.___
obvious inconsistency. This inconsistency involves the figures

    A. 50-865   B. 865-14   C. 14-02   D. 02-6

44. Ten employees were awarded merit prizes for outstanding service during the year.   44.___
Their code numbers were:

    80-345-14-04-4   40-155-12-02-2
    40-155-12-04-4   10-115-12-02-2
    10-115-13-03-2   80-115-13-02-2
    80-175-13-05-5   10-115-13-02-3
    10-115-12-04-3   30-633-14-04-4

Of these ten outstanding employees, the number who were clerks employed in the Accounting Division at a salary ranging from $24,001 to $30,000 per annum is

    A. 1   B. 2   C. 3   D. 4

45. The MOST accurate of the following statements regarding the ten outstanding employees   45.___
listed in Question 44 above is that

    A. fewer than half of the employees were under 40 years of age
    B. there were fewer typists than stenographers
    C. four of the employees were employed in the department 11 years or more
    D. two of the employees in the Research Division receive annual salaries ranging from $30,001 to $36,000

Questions 46-55.

DIRECTIONS: Questions 46 to 55 consist of groups of names. For each group, three different filing arrangements of the names in the group are given. In only one of these arrangements are the names in correct filing order according to the alphabetic filing rules which are given below. For each group, select the one arrangement, lettered A, B, or C, which is CORRECT and indicate in the space at the right the letter which corresponds to the CORRECT arrangement of names.

RULES FOR ALPHABETIC FILING

NAMES OF INDIVIDUALS

(1) The names of individuals are to be filed in strict alphabetic order. The order of filing is: first according to the last name; then according to the first name or initial; and finally according to the middle name or initial.

(2) Where two last names are identical, the one with an initial instead of the first name precedes the one with a first name beginning with the same initial letter. For example: D. Smith and D.J. Smith precede Donald Smith.

(3) Where two individuals with identical last names also have identical first names or initials, the one without a middle name or initial precedes the one with a middle name or initial. For example: D. Smith precedes D.J. Smith, and Donald Smith precedes Donald J. Smith.

(4) Where two individuals with identical last names also have identical first names or initials, the one with an initial instead of the middle name precedes the one with a middle name beginning with the same initial letter. For example: Donald J. Smith precedes Donald Joseph Smith.

NAMES OF BUSINESS ORGANIZATIONS

The names of business organizations are to be filed in alphabetic order as written, except that the names of an organization containing the name of an individual is filed alphabetically according to the name of the individual as described in the above rules. For example: John Burke Wine Co. precedes Central Storage Corp.

ADDITIONAL RULES

(1) Names composed of numerals or of abbreviations of names are to be treated as if the numerals or the abbreviations were spelled out.
(2) Prefixes such as De, Di, O', Le, and La are considered as part of the names they precede.
(3) Names beginning with "Mc" and "Mac" are to be filed as spelled.
(4) The following titles and designations are to be disregarded in filing: Dr., Mr., Jr., Sr., D.D.S., and M.D.
(5) The following are to be disregarded when they occur in the names of business organizations: the, of, and.

SAMPLE ITEM:

ARRANGEMENT A	ARRANGEMENT B	ARRANGEMENT C
Robert Morse	R. Moss	R. T. Morse
Ralph Nixon	R. T. Morse	Robert Morse
R. T. Morse	Ralph Nixon	R. Moss
R. Moss	Robert Morse	Ralph Nixon

The CORRECT arrangement is C; the answer should, therefore, be C

46. ARRANGMENT A	ARRANGEMENT B	ARRANGEMENT C 46._____
R. B. Stevens	Aled T. Stevens	R.Stevens
Chas. Stevennson	R. B. Stevens	Robert Stevens, Sr.
Robert Stevensm, Sr.	Robert Stevens, Sr.	Alfred T. Steven s
Alfred T. Stevens	Chas. Stevenson	Chas. Stevenson

47. ARRANGEMENT A	ARRANGEMENT B	ARRANGEMENT C 47._____
Mr. A. T. Breen	John Brewington	Dr. Otis C. Breen
Dr. Otis C. Breen	Amelia K. Brewington	Mr. A. T. Breen
Amelia K Brewington	Dr. Otis C. Breen	John Brewington
John Brewington	Mr. A. T. Breen	Amelia K. Brewington

12

48. ARRANGEMENT A   ARRANGEMENT B   ARRANGEMENT C   48.____
     J. Murphy   John Murphy   J. Murphy
     J. J. Murphy   John J. Murphy   John Murphy
     John Murphy   J. Murphy   J. J. Murphy
     John J. Murphy   J. J. Murphy   John J. Murphy

49. ARRANGEMENT A   ARRANGEMENT B   ARRANGEMENT C   49.____
     Anthoney Dibuono   Geo. T. Burns, Jr.   George Burns, Sr.
     George Burns, Sr   George Burns, Sr.   George T. Burns, Jr.
     Geo. T. Burns, Jr.   Anthony DiBuono   Alan J. Byrnes
     Alan J. Byrnes   Alan J. Byrnes   Anthony DiBuono

50. ARRANGEMENT A   ARRANGEMENT B   ARRANGEMENT C   50.____
     James Macauley   James Macauley   Bernard J. Macmahon
     Frank A. Mclowery   Francis Macloughry   Francis MacLaughry
     Francis Maclaughry   Bernard J.Macmahon   Frank A. McLowery
     Bernard J. MacMahon   Frank A. McLowery   James Macauley

51. ARRANGEMENT A   ARRANGEMENT B   ARRANGEMENT C   51.____
     A. J. DiBartolo, Sr.   J. A. Bartolo   Anthony J. Bartolo
     A. P.DiBartolo   Anthony J. Bartolo   J. A. Bartolo
     J. A. Bartolo   A. J. DiBartolo   A. J. DiBartolo, Sr
     Anthony J. Bartolo   A. J. DiBartolo, Sr.   A. P. DiBartolo

52. ARRANGEMENT A   ARRANGEMENT B   ARRANGEMENT C   52.____
     Edward Holmes Corp.   Edward Holmes Corp.   Hillside Trust   Corp.
     Hillside Trust Corp.   Hillside Trust Corp.   Edward Holmes Corp
     Standard Insurance Co.   The Industrial Surety Co. The Industrial Surety Co.
     The Industrial Surety Co Standard Insurance Co. Standard Insurance Co.

53. ARRANGEMENT A   ARRANGEMENT B   53.____
     Cooperative Credit Co.   Chas, Cooke Chemical Corp.
     Chas. Cooke Chemical Corp.   Cooperative Credit Co.
     John Fuller Baking Co.   4th Avenue Express Co.
     4th Avenue Express Co.   John Fuller Baking Co.

     ARRANGEMENT C
     4th Avenue Express Co.
     John Fuller Baking Co.
     Chas. Cooke Chemical Corp.
     Cooperative Credit Co.

54. ARRANGEMENT A   ARRANGEMENT B   ARRANGEMENT C   54.____
     Mr. R. McDaniels   F. L. Ramsey   Robert darling, Jr.
     Robert Darling, Jr.   Mr. R. McDaniels   Charles DeRhone
     F. L. Ramsey   Charles DeRhone   Mr. R. Mcdaniels
     Charles DeRhone   Robert Darling, Jr.   F. L. Ramsey

55.

ARRANGEMENT A	ARRANGEMENT B	ARRANGEMENT C 55._____
New York Ominibus Corp.	John J. O'Brien Co.	Nova Scotia Canning Co.
New York Shipping Co.	New York Ominibus Ciorp.	John J. O'Brien Co.
Nove Scotia Canning Co.	New York Shipping Co.	New York Ominibus Corp.
John J. O'Brien Co.	Nove Scotia Canning Co.	New York shipping Co.

56. He was asked to *pacify* the visitor. The word pacify means MOST NEARLY   56._____

    A. escort   B. interview   C. calm   D. detain

57. To say that a certain document is *authentic* means MOST NEARLY that it is   57._____

    A. fictitious   B. well written   C. priceless   D. genuine

58. A clerk who is *meticulous* in performing his work is one who is   58._____

    A. alert to improved techniques
    B. likely to be erratic and unpredictable
    C. excessively careful of small details
    D. slovenly and inaccurate

59 A pamphlet which is *replete* with charts and graphs is one which   59._____

    A. deals with the construction of charts and graphs
    B. is full of charts and graphs
    C. substitutes illustrations for tabulated data
    D. is in need of charts and graphs

60. His former secretary was *diligent* in carrying out her duties. The word diligent means   60._____
MOST NEARLY

    A. incompetent   B. cheerful   C. careless   D. industrious

61. To supepsede means MOST NEARLY to   61._____

    A. take the place of   B. come before
    C. be in charge of   D. divide into equal parts

62. He sent the *irate* employee to the pepsonnel manager. The word *irate* means   62._____
MOST NEARLY

    A. irresponsible   B. untldy   C. insubordinate   D. angry

63. An *ambiguous* statement is one which is   63._____
    A forceful and convincing
    B capable of being understood in more than one sense
    C based upon good judgment and sound reasoning processes
    D uninteresting and too lengthy

64. To *extol* means MOST NEARLY to   64.____

    A. summon   B. praise   C. reject   D. withdraw

65. The word *proximity* means MOST NEARLY   65.__

    A. similarity   B. exactness   C. harmony   D. nearness

66. His friends had a *detrimental* influence on him. The word detrimental means MOST NEARLY   66.__

    A. favorable   B. lasting   C. harmful   D. short-lived

67. The chief inspector relied upon the *veracity* of his inspectors. The word veracity means MOST NEARLY   67.__

    A. speed   B. assistance   C. shrewdness   D. truthfulness

68. There was much *diversity* in the suggestions submitted. The word diversity means MOST NEARLY   68.__

    A. similarity   B. value   C. triviality   D. variety

69. The survey was concerned with the problem of *indigence*. The word indigence means MOST NEARLY   69.__

    A. poverty   B. corruption   C. intolerance   D. morale

70. The investigator considered this evidence to be *extraneous*. The word extraneous means MOST NEARLY   70.__

    A. significant   B. pertinent but unobtainable
    C. not essential   D. inadequate

71. He was surppised at the *temerity* of the new employee. The word temerity means MOST NEARLY   71.__

    A. shyness   B. enthusiasm   C. rashness   D. self-control

72. The term *ex officio* means MOST NEARLY   72.__

    A. expelled from office
    B. a former holder of a high office
    C. without official approval
    D. by virtue of office or position

Questions 73-82.

DIRECTIONS: Questions 73 to 82 consist of four words each. One word in each row is INCORRECTLY spelled. For each item, print in the correspondingly numbered space at the right the letter preceding the word which is INCORRECTLY spelled.

73.   A. apparent   B. superintendent   C. releive   D. calendar   73.__

74.   A. foreign   B. negotiate   C. typical   D. discipline   74.__

75.   A. posponed   B. argument   C. susceptible   D. deficit   75.__

76.   A. preferred   B. column   C. peculiar   D. equiped   76.__

77.	A. exaggerate	B. disatisfied	C. repetition	D. already	77._____
78.	A. livelihood	B. physician	C. obsticle	D. strategy	78._____
79.	A. courageous	B. ommission	C. ridiculous	D. awkward	79._____
80.	A. sincerely	B. abundance	C. negligable	D. elementary	80._____
81.	A. obsolete	B. mischievous	C. enumerate	D. atheletic	81._____
82.	A. fiscel	B. beneficiary	C. concede	D. translate	82._____

Questions 83-97

DIRECTIONS: Each of the following sentences may be classified MOST appropriately under one
of the following four categories:
A. faulty because of incorrect grammar
B. faulty because of incorrect punctuation
C. faulty because of incorrect capitalization
D. correct
Examine each sentence carefully. Then, in the correspondingly numbered
space at the right, print the letter preceding the option which is the BEST of
the four suggested above. All incorrect sentences contain but one type of error.
Consider a sentence correct if it contains none of the types of errors mentioned,
even though there may be other eorrect ways of expressing the same thought.

83.   Neither of the two administrators are going to attend the conference being held in   83._____
Washington, D.C.

84.   Since Miss Smith and Miss Jones have more experience than us, they have been given   84._____
more responsible duties.

85.   Mr. Shaw the supervisor of the stock room maintains an inventory of stationery and office   85._____
supplies.

86.   Inasmuch as this matter affects both you and I, we should take joint action.   86._____

87.   Who do you think will be able to perform this highly technical work?   87._____

88.   Of the two employees, John is considered the most competent.   88._____

89.   He is not coming home on tuesday; we expect him next week.   89._____

90.   Stenographers, as well as typists must be able to type rapidly and accurately.   90._____

91.   Having been placed in the safe we were sure that the money would not be stolen   91._____

92.   Only the employees who worked overtime last week may leave one hour earlier today.   92._____

93.   We need someone who can speak french fluently.   93._____

94.   A tall, elderly, man entered the office and asked to see Mr. Brown.   94._____

95.   The clerk insisted that he had filed the correspondence in the proper cabinet.   95._____

96. "Will you assist us," he asked?   96.__

97. According to the information contained in the report, a large quantity of paper and   97.__
envelopes were used by this bureau last year.

Questions 98-100.

DIRECTIONS: Items 98 to 100 are a test of your proofreading ability.

Each item consists of Copy I and Copy II. You are to assume that Copy I in each item is correct. Copy II, which is meant to be a duplicate of Copy I, may contain some typographical errors.. In each item, compare Copy II with Copy I and determine the number of errors in Copy II. If there are:

no errors, mark your answer A;
1 or 2 errors, mark your answer B;
3 or 4 errors, mark your answer C;
5 or 6 errors, mark your answer D;
7 errors or more, mark your answer E.

98. COPY I   98.__

The Commissioner, before issuing any such license, shall cause an investigation to be made of the premises named and described in such application, to determine whether all the provisions of the sanitary code, building code, state industrial code, state minimum wage law, local laws, regulations of municipal agencies, and other requirements of this article are fully observed. (Section B32-169.0 of Article 23.)

COPY II

The Commissioner, before issuing any such license shall cause an investigation to be made of the premises named and described tn such applecation, to determine whether all the provisions of the sanitary code, bilding code, state tndustrial code, state minimum wage laws, local laws, regulations of municipal agencies, and other requirements of this article are fully observed. (Section E32-169.0 of Article 23.)

99. COPY I   99.__

Among the persons who have been appointed to various agencies are John Queen, 9 West 55th Street, Brooklyn; Joseph Blount, 2497 Durward Road, Bronx; Lawrence K. Eberhardt, 3194 Bedford Street, Manhattan; Reginald L. Darcy, 1476 Allerton Drive, Bronx; and Benjamin Ledwith, 177 Greene Street, Manhattan.

COPY II

Among the persons who have been appointed to various agencies are John Queen, 9 West 56th Street,Brooklyn, Joseph Blount, 2497 Dureward Road, Bronx; Lawrence K. Eberhart, 3194 Belford Street, Manhattan; Reginald L. Darcey, 1476 Allerton drive, Bronx; and Benjamin Ledwith, 177 Green Street, Manhattan.

100. COPY I   100.__

Except as hereinafter provided, it shall be unlawful to use, store or have on hand any inflammable motion picture film in quantities greater than one standard or two sub-standard reels, or aggregating more than two thousand feet in length, or more than ten pounds in weight without the permit required by this section.

COPY II

Except as herinafter provided, it shall be unlawfull to use, store or have on hand any inflammable motion picture film, in quantities greater than one standard or two substandard reels or aggregating more than two thousand feet in length, or more than ten pounds in weight without the permit required by this section.

17

KEY (CORRECT ANSWERS)

1. C	26. D	51. C	76. D
2. D	27. A	52. C	77. B
3. B	28. C	53. B	78. C
4. D	29. D	54. C	79. B
5. A	30. C	55. A	80. C
6. B	31. A	56. C	81. D
7. C	32. C	57. D	82. A
8. C	33. B	58. C	83. A
9. A	34. D	59. B	84. A
10. B	35. B	60. D	85. B
11. A	36. B	61. A	86. A
12. C	37. C	62. D	87. D
13. D	38. A	63. B	88. A
14. A	39. B	64. B	89. C
15. B	40. B	65. D	90. B
16. D	41. D	66. C	91. A
17. C	42. A	67. D	92. D
18. B	43. D	68. D	93. C
19. C	44. B	69. A	94. B
20. D	45. C	70. C	95. D
21. B	46. B	71. C	96. B
22. A	47. A	72. D	97. A
23. A	48. A	73. C	98. D
24. D	49. C	74. D	99. E
25. B	50. B	75. A	100. E

EXAMINATION SECTION
TEST 1

DIRECTIONS: Each question or incomplete statement is followed by several suggested answers or completions. Select the one that BEST answers the question or completes the statement. *PRINT THE LETTER OF THE CORRECT ANSWER IN THE SPACE AT THE RIGHT.*

1. The CHIEF assumption underlying the provisions for a salary range with a minimum, a maximum, and intervening steps for each class in the compensation plans of MOST public agencies is that

   A. the granting of periodic increments to employees encourages staff stability at the lowest possible cost
   B. job offers made at a step higher than the minimum of a salary range are a positive aid to recruitment
   C. automatic salary increments provide an incentive to employees to improve their job performances from year to year
   D. an employee's value to his employer tends to increase with the passage of time

1.____

2. Selection of candidates for employment on the basis of aptitude test results is made on the assumption that the candidates making the highest test scores

   A. possess the most knowledge about the job for which they were tested
   B. will need a minimum amount of training on the job for which they were tested
   C. will be the most satisfactory employees after they have received training
   D. are those who will have the highest interest in succeeding on the job for which they were tested

2.____

3. In position classification, the one of the following factors which is of LEAST importance in classifying a clerical position is the

   A. degree of supervision under which the work of the position is performed
   B. amount of supervision exercised over other positions
   C. training and experience of the incumbent of the position
   D. extent to which independent judgment must be exercised in performing the duties of the position

3.____

4. The position classifying bureau of the central personnel agency in a public jurisdiction is normally NOT responsible for

   A. allocating individual positions to classes
   B. assigning titles to classes of positions
   C. establishing minimum qualifications for positions
   D. determining which positions are necessary

4.____

5. The one of the following which is generally considered to be an ESSENTIAL element in the process of classifying a position in a civil service system is the

   A. comparison of the position with similar and related positions
   B. evaluation of the skill with which the duties of the position are being performed
   C. number of positions similar to the position being classified
   D. determination of the salary being paid for the position

5.____

6. Of the following, the LEAST important objective of a modern service rating system which is applied to civil service positions is to   6.___

   A. validate selection procedures
   B. improve the quality of supervision
   C. furnish a basis for the construction of a position classification plan
   D. foster the development of good employee performance

7. Some public agencies conduct exit interviews with employees who quit their jobs. The one of the following which is generally considered to be the CHIEF value to a public agency of such an interview is in   7.___

   A. ascertaining from the employee the reasons why he is leaving his job
   B. obtaining reliable information on the employee's work history with the agency
   C. persuading the employee to reconsider his decision to quit
   D. giving the employee a final evaluation of his work performance

8. The rate of labor turnover in an organization may be arrived at by dividing the total number of separations from the organization in a given period by the average number of workers employed in the same period. In arriving at the rate, it is assumed that those separated are replaced.
If the rate of turnover is excessively low in comparison with other similar organizations, it USUALLY indicates that   8.___

   A. the organization is stagnant
   B. promotions within the organization are made frequently
   C. the organization's recruitment policies have been ineffective
   D. suitable workers are in short supply

9. Of the following aspects of a training program for supervisory personnel in a public agency, the aspect for which it is usually the MOST difficult to develop adequate information is the   9.___

   A. determination of the training needs of the supervisory personnel in the agency
   B. establishment of the objectives of the program
   C. selection of suitable training methods for the program
   D. evaluation of the effectiveness of the training program

10. You are conducting a training conference for new supervisors on supervisory techniques and problems. When one of the participants in the conference proposes what you consider to be an unsatisfactory solution for the problem under discussion, none of the other participants questions the solution or offers an alternate solution.
For you to tell the group why the solution is unsatisfactory would be   10.___

   A. *desirable* chiefly because satisfactory rather than unsatisfactory solutions to the problems should be stressed in the conference
   B. *undesirable* chiefly because the participants them-selves should be stimulated to present reasons why the proposed solution is unsatisfactory
   C. *desirable* chiefly because you, as the conference leader, should guide the participants in solving conference problems
   D. *undesirable* chiefly because the proposed unsatisfactory solution may be useful in illustrating the advantages of a satisfactory solution

11. It is generally BEST that the greater part of in-service training for the operating employ-   11.____
     ees of an agency in a public jurisdiction be given by

     A. a team of trainers from the central personnel agency of the jurisdiction
     B. training specialists on the staff of the personnel unit of the agency
     C. a team of teachers from the public school system of the jurisdiction
     D. members of the regular supervisory force of the agency

12. You are responsible for training a number of your subordinates to handle some compli-   12.____
     cated procedures which your unit will adopt after the training has been completed. If
     approximately 30 hours of training are required and you can arrange the training ses-
     sions during working hours as you see fit, learning would ordinarily be BEST effected if
     you scheduled the trainees to devote _____ to the training until it is completed.

     A. a half day each week   B. one full day each week
     C. a half day every day   D. full time

13. Assume that you are giving a lecture for the purpose of explaining a new procedure. You   13.____
     find that the employees attending the lecture are asking many questions on the material
     as you present it. Consequently, you realize that you will be unable to cover all of the
     material you had intended to cover, and that a second lecture will be necessary.
     In this situation, the MOST advisable course of action for you to take would be to

     A. answer the questions on the new procedure as they arise
     B. answer the questions that can be answered quickly and ask the employees to
         reserve questions requiring lengthier answers for the second lecture
     C. suggest that further questions be withheld until the second lecture so that you can
         cover as much of the remaining material as possible
     D. refer the questions back to the employees asking them

14. As a supervisor, you are conducting a training conference dealing with administrative   14.____
     principles and practices.
     One of the members of the conference, Mr. Smith, makes a factual statement which
     you know to be incorrect and which may hinder the development of the discussion.
     None of the other members attempts to correct Mr. Smith or to question him on what
     he has said, although until this point, the members have participated actively in the dis-
     cussions. In this situation, the MOST advisable course of action for you to take would
     be to

     A. proceed with the discussion without commenting on Mr. Smith's statement
     B. correct the statement that Mr. Smith has made
     C. emphasize that the material discussed at the conference is to serve only as a
         guide for handling actual work situations
     D. urge the members to decide for themselves whether or not to accept factual state-
         ments made at the conference

15. With the wholehearted support of top management, the training bureau of a public   15.___
agency schedules a series of training conferences for all the supervisory and administrative employees in order to alter their approaches to the problems arising from the inter-
action of supervisors and subordinates. During the conferences, the participants discuss
solutions to typical problems of this type and become conscious of the principles underlying these solutions. After the series of conferences is concluded, it is found that the
first-line supervisors are not applying the principles to the problems they are encounter-
ing on the job.
Of the following, the MOST likely reason why these supervisors are not putting the
principles into practice is that

    A. the training conferences have not changed the attitudes of these supervisors
    B. these supervisors are reluctant to put into practice methods with which their subor-
dinates are unfamiliar
    C. the conference method is not suitable for human relations training
    D. the principles which were covered in the conferences are not suitable for solving
actual work problems

16. Assume that you are the leader of a training conference dealing with supervisory tech-   16.___
niques and problems. One of the problems being discussed is one with which you have
had no experience, but two of the participants have had considerable experience with it.
These two participants carry on an extended discussion of the problem in light of their
experiences, and it is obvious from their discussion that they understand the problem
thoroughly. It is also obvious that the other participants in the conference are very much
interested in the discussion and are taking notes on the material presented.
For you to permit the two participants to continue until the amount of time allowed for
discussion of the problem has been exhausted would be

    A. *desirable* chiefly because their discussion, which is based on actual work experi-
ence, may be more meaningful to the other participants than would a discussion
which is not based on work experience
    B. *undesirable* chiefly because they are discussing the material only in the light of
their own experiences rather than in general terms
    C. *desirable* chiefly because the introduction of the material by two of the participants
themselves may put the other participants at ease
    D. *undesirable* chiefly because the other participants are not joining in the discussion
of the problem

17. You are a supervisor in charge of a unit of clerical employees. One of your subordinates,   17.___
Mr. Smith, has not seemed to be his usual self in the past several weeks, but rather has
seemed to be disturbed. In addition, he has not been producing his usual quantity of
work and has been provoking arguments with his colleagues. He approaches you and
asks if he may discuss with you a problem which he believes has been affecting his work.
As Mr. Smith begins to discuss the problem, you immediately realize that, although it may
be disturbing to him, it is really a trivial matter.
Of the following, the FIRST step that you should take in this situation is to

    A. permit Mr. Smith to continue to describe his problem, interrupting him only when
clarification of a point is needed
    B. tell Mr. Smith that his becoming unduly upset about the problem will not help to
solve it

C. point out that you and your subordinates have faced more serious problems and that this one is a relatively minor matter
D. suggest that the problem should be solved before it develops into a serious matter

18. A line supervisor can play an important role in helping his subordinates to make healthy mental, emotional, and social adjustments.
The one of the following which would NOT be considered to be a part of the supervisor's role in helping his subordinates to make these adjustments is to

18.____

A. ascertain which subordinates are likely to develop maladjustments
B. recognize indications of these types of maladjustments
C. refer subordinates displaying signs of maladjustments that he cannot handle to specialists for assistance
D. create a work environment that will tend to minimize his subordinates' preoccupations with personal problems

19. One of the principal duties of the management in a public agency is to secure the most effective utilization of personnel.
The one of the following which would contribute LEAST to effective utilization and development of personnel in a public agency is

19.____

A. the use of training programs designed to prepare employees for future tasks
B. a comprehensive list of skills and abilities needed to perform the work of the agency effectively
C. a systematic effort to discover employees of high potential and to develop them for future responsibilities
D. the assignment of employees to duties which require the maximum use of their abilities

20. During a training session for new employees, an employee becomes upset because he is unable to solve a problem presented to him by the instructor.
Of the following actions which the instructor could take, the one which would be MOST likely to dispel the employee's emotional state is to

20.____

A. give him a different type of problem which he may be able to solve
B. minimize the importance of finding a solution to the problem and proceed to the next topic
C. encourage the other participants to contribute to the solution
D. provide him with hints which would enable him to solve the problem

21. Studies in human behavior have shown that an employee in a work group who is capable of producing substantially more work than is being produced by the average of the group GENERALLY will

21.____

A. tend to produce substantially more work than is produced by the average member of the group
B. attempt to become the informal leader of the group
C. tend to produce less work than he is capable of producing
D. attempt to influence the other members of the group to increase their production

22. Studies of organizations show that formal employee participation in the formulation of work policies before they are put into effect is MOST likely to result in a(n)   22.___

    A. reduction in the length of time required to formulate the policies
    B. increase in the number of employees affected by the policies
    C. reduction in the length of time required to implement the policies
    D. increase in the number of policies formulated within the organization

23. No matter how elaborate a formal system of communication is in an organization, the system will always be supplemented by informal channels of communication, such as the *grapevine*. Although such informal channels of communication are usually not highly regarded, they sometimes are of value to an organization.
Of the following, the CHIEF value of informal channels of communication is that they serve to   23.___

    A. transmit information that management has neglected to send through the formal system of communication
    B. confirm information that has already been received through the formal system of communication
    C. hinder the formation of employee cliques in the organization
    D. revise information sent through the formal system of communication

24. The one of the following which is generally considered to be the MOST important advantage of the written questionnaire method of obtaining information is that this method   24.___

    A. assures accuracy of response greater than that obtained from other methods
    B. gives the persons to whom the questionnaire is sent the opportunity to express their opinions and feelings
    C. makes it possible to obtain the responses of many persons at small cost
    D. permits errors in the information obtained to be corrected easily when they are discovered

25. In collecting objective data for the evaluation of procedures which are used in his agency, an administrator should, in every case, be careful   25.___

    A. to take an equal number of measurements from each source of information
    B. not to allow his beliefs about the values of the procedures to influence the choice of data
    C. to apply statistical methods continuously to the data as they are gathered to assure maximum accuracy
    D. not to accept data which are inconsistent with the general trend established by verified data

KEY CORRECT ANSWERS

1.	D		11.	D
2.	C		12.	C
3.	C		13.	A
4.	D		14.	B
5.	A		15.	A
6.	C		16.	D
7.	A		17.	A
8.	A		18.	A
9.	D		19.	B
10.	B		20.	D

21.	C
22.	C
23.	A
24.	C
25.	B

TEST 2

DIRECTIONS: Each question or incomplete statement is followed by several suggested answers or completions. Select the one that BEST answers the question or completes the statement. *PRINT THE LETTER OF THE CORRECT ANSWER IN THE SPACE AT THE RIGHT*

1. Assume that the law enforcement division in a public jurisdiction employs only males who are 5 feet 8 inches or taller.
   To expect the heights of these employees to be normally distributed is UNJUSTIFIED primarily because

   A. the distribution of a random sample is not usually the same as the distribution of the population from which the sample was drawn
   B. no maximum height requirement has been established
   C. height is a characteristic which is not normally distributed in the general population of males
   D. the employees are not a representative sample of the general population of males

1.___

Questions 2-5.

DIRECTIONS: Questions 2 through 5 are to be answered SOLELY on the basis of the information contained in the following paragraph.

A standard comprises characteristics attached to an aspect of a process or product by which it can be evaluated. Standardization is the development and adoption of standards. When they are formulated, standards are not usually the product of a single person, but represent the thoughts and ideas of a group, leavened with the knowledge and information which are currently available. Standards which do not meet certain basic requirements become a hindrance rather than an aid to progress. Standards must not only be correct, accurate, and precise in requiring no more and no less than what is needed for satisfactory results, but they must also be workable in the sense that their usefulness is not nullified by external conditions. Standards should also be acceptable to the people who use them. If they are not acceptable, they cannot be considered to be satisfactory, although they may possess all the other essential characteristics.

2. According to the above paragraph, a processing standard that requires the use of materials that cannot be procured is MOST likely to be

   A. incomplete   B. inaccurate
   C. unworkable   D. unacceptable

2.___

3. According to the above paragraph, the construction of standards to which the performance of job duties should conform is MOST often

   A. the work of the people responsible for seeing that the duties are properly performed
   B. accomplished by the person who is best informed about the functions involved
   C. the responsibility of the people who are to apply them
   D. attributable to the efforts of various informed persons

3.___

4. According to the above paragraph, when standards call for finer tolerances than those essential to the conduct of successful production operations, the effect of the standards on the improvement of production operations is   4.____

   A. negative   B. nullified
   C. negligible   D. beneficial

5. The one of the following which is the MOST suitable title for the above paragraph is   5.____

   A. The Evaluation of Formulated Standards
   B. The Attributes of Satisfactory Standards
   C. The Adoption of Acceptable Standards
   D. The Use of Process or Product Standards

Questions 6-9.

DIRECTIONS: Questions 6 through 9 are to be answered SOLELY on the basis of the infor-
               mation contained in the following paragraph.

Good personnel relations of an organization depend upon mutual confidence, trust, and good will. The basis of confidence is understanding. Most troubles start with people who do not understand each other. When the organization 's intentions or motives are misunderstood, or when reasons for actions, practices, or policies are misconstrued, complete cooperation from individuals is not forthcoming. If management expects full cooperation from employees, it has a responsibility of sharing with them the information which is the foundation of proper understanding, confidence, and trust. Personnel management has long since outgrown the days when it was the vogue to treat them rough and tell them nothing. Up-to-date personnel management provides all possible information about the activities, aims, and purposes of the organization. It seems altogether creditable that a desire should exist among employees for such information which the best-intentioned executive might think, would not interest them and which the worst-intentioned would think was none of their business.

6. The above paragraph implies that one of the causes of the difficulty which an organization might have with its personnel relations is that its employees   6.____

   A. have not expressed interest in the activities, aims, and purposes of the organization
   B. do not believe in the good faith of the organization
   C. have not been able to give full cooperation to the organization
   D. do not recommend improvements in the practices and policies of the organization

7. According to the above paragraph, in order for an organization to have good personnel relations, it is NOT essential that   7.____

   A. employees have confidence in the organization
   B. the purposes of the organization be understood by the employees
   C. employees have a desire for information about the organization
   D. information about the organization be communicated to employees

8. According to the paragraph, an organization which provides full information about itself to   8.___
its employees

    A. understands the intentions of its employees
    B. satisfies a praiseworthy desire among its employees
    C. is managed by executives who have the best intentions toward its employees
    D. is confident that its employees understand its motives

9. The one of the following which is the MOST suitable title for the paragraph is   9.___

    A. The Foundations of Personnel Relations
    B. The Consequences of Employee Misunderstanding
    C. The Development of Personnel Management Practices
    D. The Acceptance of Organizational Objectives

Questions 10-13.

DIRECTIONS: Questions 10 through 13 are to be answered SOLELY on the basis of the information contained in the following paragraph.

*Management, which is the function of executive leadership, has as its principal phases
the planning, organizing, and controlling of the activities of subordinate groups in the accomplishment of organizational objectives. Planning specifies the kind and extent of the factors,
forces, and effects, and the relationships among them, that will be required for satisfactory
accomplishment. The nature of the objectives and their requirements must be known before
determinations can be made as to what must be done, how it must be done and why, where
actions should take place, who should be responsible, and similar problems pertaining to the
formulation of a plan. Organizing, which creates the conditions that must be present before
the execution of the plan can be undertaken successfully, cannot be done intelligently without
knowledge of the organizational objectives. Control, which has to do with the constraint and
regulation of activities entering into the execution of the plan, must be exercised in accordance with the characteristics and requirements of the activities demanded by the plan.*

10. The one of the following which is the MOST suitable title for the paragraph is   10.___

    A. The Nature of Successful Organization
    B. The Planning of Management Functions
    C. The Importance of Organizational Objectives
    D. The Principle Aspects of Management

11. It can be inferred from the paragraph that the one of the following functions whose exist-   11.___
ence is essential to the existence of the other three is the

    A. regulation of the work needed to carry out a plan
    B. understanding of what the organization intends to accomplish
    C. securing of information of the factors necessary for accomplishment of objectives
    D. establishment of the conditions required for successful action

12. The one of the following which would NOT be included within any of the principal phases   12.____
of the function of executive leadership as defined in the paragraph is

   A. determination of manpower requirements
   B. procurement of required material
   C. establishment of organizational objectives
   D. scheduling of production

13. The conclusion which can MOST reasonably be drawn from the paragraph is that the   13.____
control phase of managing is most directly concerned with the

   A. influencing of policy determinations
   B. administering of suggestion systems
   C. acquisition of staff for the organization
   D. implementation of performance standards

14. A study reveals that Miss Brown files N cards in M hours, and Miss Smith files the same   14.____
number of cards in T hours. If the two employees work together, the number of hours it
will take them to file N cards is

A. $\dfrac{N}{\dfrac{N}{M}+\dfrac{N}{T}}$

B. $\dfrac{N}{T+M}+\dfrac{2N}{MT}$

C. $N\left(\dfrac{M}{N}+\dfrac{N}{T}\right)$

D. $\dfrac{N}{NT+MN}$

Questions 15-20.

DIRECTIONS: Questions 15 through 20 are to be answered SOLELY on the basis of the information contained in the five charts below which relate to Bureau X in a City
Department. The Bureau has an office in each of the five boroughs.

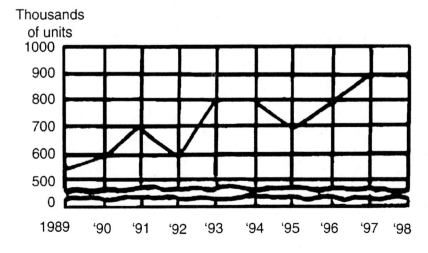

NUMBER OF UNITS OF WORK PRODUCED IN
THE BUREAU PER YEAR

INCREASE IN THE NUMBER OF UNITS OF WORK PRODUCED IN 1998 OVER THE NUMBER PRODUCED IN 1989, BY BOROUGH

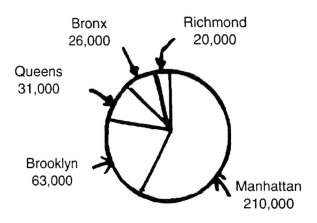

Bronx
26,000

Richmond
20,000

Queens
31,000

Brooklyn
63,000

Manhattan
210,000

NUMBER OF MALE AND FEMALE EMPLOYEES PRODUCING THE UNITS OF WORK THE BUREAU PER YEAR

Number of Employees

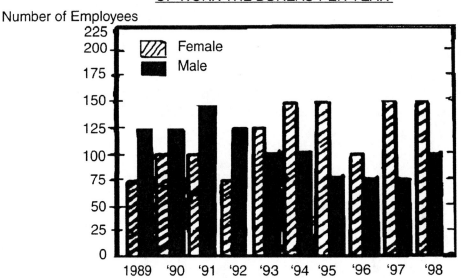

DISTRIBUTION OF THE AGES BY PER CENT, OF EMPLOYEES
ASSIGNED TO PRODUCE THE UNITS OF WORK IN THE YEARS
1989 AND 1998

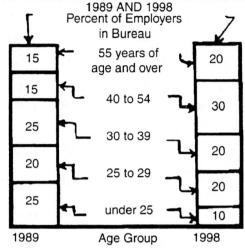

TOTAL SALARIES PAID PER YEAR TO EMPLOYEES ASSIGNED
TO PRODUCE THE UNITS OF WORK IN THE BUREAU

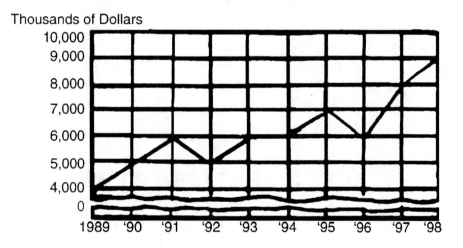

15. The information contained in the charts is sufficient to determine the   15.____

   A. amount of money paid in salaries to employees working in Richmond in 1998
   B. difference between the average annual salary of employees in the Bureau in 1998
      and their average annual salary in 1997
   C. number of female employees in the Bureau between 30 and 39 years of age who
      were employed in 1989
   D. cost, in salary, for the average male employee in the Bureau to produce 100 units
      of work in 1994

16. The one of the following which was GREATER in the Bureau in 1994 than it was in 1992 was the

16.___

   A. cost, in salaries, of producing a unit of work
   B. units of work produced annually per employee
   C. proportion of female employees to total number of employees
   D. average annual salary per employee

17. If, in 1998, one-half of the employees in the Bureau 55 years of age and over each earned an annual salary of $42,000, then the average annual salary of all the remaining employees in the Bureau was MOST NEARLY

17.___

   A. $31,750   B. $34,500   C. $35,300   D. $35,800

18. Assume that, in 1989, the offices in Richmond and the Bronx each produced the same number of units of work. Also assume that, in 1989, the offices in Brooklyn, Manhattan, and Queens each produced twice as many units of work as were produced in either of the other two boroughs.
Then, the number of units of work produced in Brooklyn in 1998 was MOST NEARLY

18.___

   A. 69,000   B. 138,000   C. 201,000   D. 225,000

19. If, in 1996, the average annual salary of the female employees in the Bureau was four-fifths as large as the average annual salary of the male employees, then the average annual salary of the female employees in that year was

19.___

   A. $37,500   B. $31,000   C. $30,500   D. $30,000

20. Of the total number of employees in the Bureau who were 30 years of age and over in 1989,

20.___

   A. at least 35 must have been females
   B. less than 75 must have been males
   C. no more than 100 must have been females
   D. more than 15 must have been males

KEY (CORRECT ANSWERS)

1.	D	11.	B
2.	C	12.	C
3.	D	13.	D
4.	A	14.	A
5.	B	15.	B
6.	B	16.	B
7.	C	17.	C
8.	B	18.	C
9.	A	19.	D
10.	D	20.	A

READING COMPREHENSION
UNDERSTANDING AND INTERPRETING WRITTEN MATERIAL
EXAMINATION SECTION
TEST 1

DIRECTIONS: Each question or incomplete statement is followed by several suggested
answers or completions. Select the one that BEST answers the question or
completes the statement. *PRINT THE LETTER OF THE CORRECT ANSWER
IN THE SPACE AT THE RIGHT.*

Questions 1-2.

DIRECTIONS: Questions 1 and 2 are to be answered SOLELY on the basis of the following
passage.

The employees in a unit or division of a government agency may be referred to as a work
group. Within a government agency which has existed for some time, the work groups will
have evolved traditions of their own. The persons in these work groups acquire these traditions as part of the process of work adjustment within their groups. Usually, a work group in a
large organization will contain *oldtimers, newcomers,* and *in-betweeners.* Like the supervisor
of a group, who is not necessarily an oldtimer or the oldest member, oldtimers usually have
great influence. They can recall events unknown to others and are a storehouse of information and advice about current problems in the light of past experience. They pass along the
traditions of the group to the others who, in turn, become oldtimers themselves. Thus, the traditions of the group which have been honored and revered by long acceptance are continued.

1. According to the above passage, the traditions of a work group within a government   1.____
    agency are developed

    A. at the time the group is established
    B. over a considerable period of time
    C. in order to give recognition to oldtimers
    D. for the group before it is established

2. According to the above passage, the oldtimers within a work group   2.____

    A. are the means by which long accepted practices and customs are perpetuated
    B. would best be able to settle current problems that arise
    C. are honored because of the changes they have made in the traditions
    D. have demonstrated that they have learned to do their work well

Questions 3-4.

DIRECTIONS: Questions 3 and 4 are to be answered SOLELY on the basis of the following
passage.

In public agencies, the success of a person assigned to perform first-line supervisory duties depends in large part upon the personal relations between him and his subordinate employees. The goal of supervising effort is something more than to obtain compliance with procedures established by some central office. The major objective is work accomplishment. In order for this goal to be attained, employees must want to attain it and must exercise initiative in their work. Only if employees are generally satisfied with the type of supervision which exists in an organization will they put forth their best efforts.

3. According to the above passage, in order for employees to try to do their work as well as they can, it is essential that

    A. they participate in determining their working conditions and rates of pay
    B. their supervisors support the employees' viewpoints in meetings with higher management
    C. they are content with the supervisory practices which are being used
    D. their supervisors make the changes in working procedures that the employees request

4. It can be inferred from the above passage that the goals of a unit in a public agency will not be reached unless the employees in the unit

    A. wish to reach them and are given the opportunity to make individual contributions to the work
    B. understand the relationship between the goals of the unit and goals of the agency
    C. have satisfactory personal relationships with employees of other units in the agency
    D. carefully follow the directions issued by higher authorities

Questions 5-9.

DIRECTIONS: Questions 5 through 9 are to be answered SOLELY on the basis of the following passage.

If an employee thinks he can save money, time, or material for the city or has an idea about how to do something better than it is being done, he shouldn't keep it to himself. He should send his ideas to the Employees' Suggestion Program, using the special form which is kept on hand in all departments. An employee may send in as many ideas as he wishes. To make sure that each idea is judged fairly, the name of the suggester is not made known until an award is made. The awards are certificates of merit or cash prizes ranging from $10 to $500.

5. According to the above passage, an employee who knows how to do a job in a better way should

    A. be sure it saves enough time to be worthwhile
    B. get paid the money he saves for the city
    C. keep it to himself to avoid being accused of causing a speed-up
    D. send his idea to the Employees' Suggestion Program

6. In order to send his idea to the Employees' Suggestion Program, an employee should   6.____

    A. ask the Department of Personnel for a special form
    B. get the special form in his own department
    C. mail the idea using Special Delivery
    D. send it on plain, white letter-size paper

7. An employee may send to the Employees' Suggestion Program   7.____

    A. as many ideas as he can think of
    B. no more than one idea each week
    C. no more than ten ideas in a month
    D. only one idea on each part of the job

8. The reason the name of an employee who makes a suggestion is not made known at first   8.____
is to

    A. give the employee a larger award
    B. help the judges give more awards
    C. insure fairness in judging
    D. only one idea on each part of the job

9. An employee whose suggestion receives an award may be given a   9.____

    A. bonus once a year   B. certificate for $10
    C. cash prize of up to $500   D. salary increase of $500

Questions 10-12.

DIRECTIONS: Questions 10 through 12 are to be answered SOLELY on the basis of the following passage.

According to the rules of the Department of Personnel, the work of every permanent city employee is reviewed and rated by his supervisor at least once a year. The civil service rating system gives the employee and his supervisor a chance to talk about the progress made during the past year as well as about those parts of the job in which the employee needs to do better. In order to receive a pay increase each year, the employee must have a satisfactory service rating. Service ratings also count toward an employee's final mark on a promotion examination.

10. According to the above passage, a permanent city employee is rated AT LEAST once   10.____

    A. before his work is reviewed
    B. every six months
    C. yearly by his supervisor
    D. yearly by the Department of Personnel

11. According to the above passage, under the rating system the supervisor and the   11.____
employee can discuss how

    A. much more work needs to be done next year
    B. the employee did his work last year

C. the work can be made easier next year
D. the work of the Department can be increased

12. According to the above passage, a permanent city employee will NOT receive a yearly pay increase   12.___

A. if he received a pay increase the year before
B. if he used his service rating for his mark on a promotion examination
C. if his service rating is unsatisfactory
D. unless he got some kind of a service rating

Questions 13-16.

DIRECTIONS: Questions 13 through 16 are to be answered SOLELY on the basis of the following passage.

It is an accepted fact that the rank and file employee can frequently advance worthwhile suggestions toward increasing efficiency. For this reason, an Employees' Suggestion System has been developed and put into operation. Suitable means have been provided at each departmental location for the confidential submission of suggestions. Numerous suggestions have been received thus far and, after study, about five percent of the ideas submitted are being translated into action. It is planned to set up, eventually, monetary awards for all worthwhile suggestions.

13. According to the above passage, a MAJOR reason why an Employees' Suggestion System was established is that   13.___

A. an organized program of improvement is better than a haphazard one
B. employees can often give good suggestions to increase efficiency
C. once a fact is accepted, it is better to act on it than to do nothing
D. the suggestions of rank and file employees were being neglected

14. According to the above passage, under the Employees' Suggestion System,   14.___

A. a file of worthwhile suggestions will eventually be set up at each departmental location
B. it is possible for employees to turn in suggestions without fellow employees knowing of it
C. means have been provided for the regular and frequent collection of suggestions submitted
D. provision has been made for the judging of worthwhile suggestions by an Employees' Suggestion Committee

15. According to the above passage, it is reasonable to assume that   15.___

A. all suggestions must be turned in at a central office
B. employees who make worthwhile suggestions will be promoted
C. not all the prizes offered will be monetary ones
D. prizes of money will be given for the best suggestions

16. According to the above passage, of the many suggestions made,   16._____

    A. all are first tested
    B. a small part are put into use
    C. most are very worthwhile
    D. samples are studied

Questions 17-20.

DIRECTIONS: Questions 17 through 20 are to be answered SOLELY on the basis of the following passage.

Employees may be granted leaves of absence without pay at the discretion of the Personnel Officer. Such a leave without pay shall begin on the first working day on which the employee does not report for duty and shall continue to the first day on which the employee returns to duty. The Personnel Division may vary the dates of the leave for the record so as to conform with payroll periods, but in no case shall an employee be off the payroll for a different number of calendar days than would have been the case if the actual dates mentioned above had been used. An employee who has vacation or overtime to his credit, which is available for normal use, may take time off immediately prior to beginning a leave of absence without pay, chargeable against all or part of such vacation or overtime.

17. According to the above passage, the Personnel Officer must   17._____

    A. decide if a leave of absence without pay should be granted
    B. require that a leave end on the last working day of a payroll period
    C. see to it that a leave of absence begins on the first working day of a pay period
    D. vary the dates of a leave of absence to conform with a payroll period

18. According to the above passage, the exact dates of a leave of absence without pay may be varied provided that the   18._____

    A. calendar days an employee is off the payroll equal the actual leave granted
    B. leave conforms to an even number of payroll periods
    C. leave when granted made provision for variance to simplify payroll records
    D. Personnel Officer approves the variation

19. According to the above passage, a leave of absence without pay must extend from the   19._____

    A. first day of a calendar period to the first day the employee resumes work
    B. first day of a payroll period to the last calendar day of the leave
    C. first working day missed to the first day on which the employee resumes work
    D. last day on which an employee works through the first day he returns to work

20. According to the above passage, an employee may take extra time off just before the start of a leave of absence without pay if   20._____

    A. he charges this extra time against his leave
    B. he has a favorable balance of vacation or overtime which has been frozen
    C. the vacation or overtime that he would normally use for a leave without pay has not been charged in this way before
    D. there is time to his credit which he may use

Question 21.

DIRECTIONS: Question 21 is to be answered SOLELY on the basis of the following passage.

In considering those things which are motivators and incentives to work, it might be just as erroneous not to give sufficient weight to money as an incentive as it is to give too much weight. It is not a problem of establishing a rank-order of importance, but one of knowing that motivation is a blend or mixture rather than a pure element. It is simple to say that cultural factors count more than financial considerations, but this leads only to the conclusion that our society is financial-oriented.

21.   Based on the above passage, in our society, cultural and social motivations to work are   21.___

    A.   things which cannot be avoided
    B.   melded to financial incentives
    C.   of less consideration than high pay
    D.   not balanced equally with economic or financial considerations

Question 22.

DIRECTIONS: Question 22 is to be answered SOLELY on the basis of the following passage.

A general principle of training and learning with respect to people is that they learn more readily if they receive *feedback*. Essential to maintaining proper motivational levels is knowledge of results which indicate level of progress. Feedback also assists the learning process by identifying mistakes. If this kind of information were not given to the learner, then improper or inappropriate job performance may be instilled.

22.   Based on the above passage, which of the following is MOST accurate?   22.___

    A.   Learning will not take place without feedback.
    B.   In the absence of feedback, improper or inappropriate job performance will be learned.
    C.   To properly motivate a learner, the learner must have his progress made known to him.
    D.   Trainees should be told exactly what to do if they are to learn properly.

Question 23.

DIRECTIONS: Question 23 is to be answered SOLELY on the basis of the following passage.

In a democracy, the obligation of public officials is twofold. They must not only do an efficient and satisfactory job of administration, but also they must persuade the public that it is an efficient and satisfactory job. It is a burden which, if properly assumed, will make democracy work and perpetuate reform government.

23.   The above passage means that   23.___

    A.   public officials should try to please everybody
    B.   public opinion is instrumental in determining the policy of public officials

C. satisfactory performance of the job of administration will eliminate opposition to its work
D. frank and open procedure in a public agency will aid in maintaining progressive government

Question 24.

DIRECTIONS: Question 24 is to be answered SOLELY on the basis of the following passage.

Upon retirement for service, a member shall receive a retirement allowance which shall consist of an annuity which shall be the actuarial equivalent of his accumulated deductions at the time of his retirement and a pension, in addition to his annuity, which shall be equal to one service-fraction of his final compensation, multiplied by the number of years of service since he last became a member credited to him, and a pension which is the actuarial equivalent of the reserve-for-increased-take-home-pay to which he may then be entitled, if any.

24. According to the above passage, a retirement allowance shall consist of a(n)   24.____

A. annuity, plus a pension, plus an actuarial equivalent
B. annuity, plus a pension, plus reserve-for-increased-take-home-pay, if any
C. annuity, plus reserve-for-increased-take-home-pay, if any, plus final compensation
D. pension, plus reserve-for-increased-take-home-pay, if any, plus accumulated deductions

Question 25.

DIRECTIONS: Question 25 is to be answered SOLELY on the basis of the following passage.

Membership in the retirement system shall cease upon the occurrence of any one of the following conditions: when the time out of service of any member who has total service of less than 25 years, shall aggregate more than 5 years; when the time out of service of any member who has total service of 25 years or more, shall aggregate more than 10 years; when any member shall have withdrawn more than 50% of his accumulated deductions; or when any member shall have withdrawn the cash benefit provided by Section B3-35.0 of the Administrative Code.

25. According to the information in the above passage, membership in the retirement system   25.____
shall cease when an employee

A. with 17 years of service has been on a leave of absence for 3 years
B. withdraws 50% of his accumulated deductions
C. with 28 years of service has been out of service for 10 years
D. withdraws his cash benefits

KEY (CORRECT ANSWERS)

1.	B		11.	B
2.	A		12.	C
3.	C		13.	B
4.	A		14.	B
5.	D		15.	D
6.	B		16.	B
7.	A		17.	A
8.	C		18.	A
9.	B		19.	C
10.	C		20.	D

21.	B
22.	C
23.	D
24.	B
25.	D

———

TEST 2

DIRECTIONS: Each question or incomplete statement is followed by several suggested answers or completions. Select the one that BEST answers the question or completes the statement. *PRINT THE LETTER OF THE CORRECT ANSWER IN THE SPACE AT THE RIGHT.*

Questions 1-6.

DIRECTIONS: Questions 1 through 6 are to be answered SOLELY on the basis of the following passage from an old office manual.

Since almost every office has some contact with data-processed records, a stenographer should have some understanding of the basic operations of data processing. Data processing systems now handle about one-third of all office paperwork. On punched cards, magnetic tape, or on other mediums, data are recorded before being fed into the computer for processing. A machine such as the keypunch is used to convert the data written on the source document into the coded symbols on punched cards or tapes. After data has been converted, it must be verified to guarantee absolute accuracy of conversion. In this manner, data becomes a permanent record which can be read by electronic computers that compare, store, compute, and otherwise process data at high speeds.

One key person in a computer installation is a programmer, the man or woman who puts business and scientific problems into special symbolic languages that can be read by the computer. Jobs done by the computer range all the way from payroll operations to chemical process control, but most computer applications are directed toward management data. About half of the programmers employed by business come to their positions with college degrees; the remaining half are promoted to their positions from within the organization on the basis of demonstrated ability without regard to education.

1. Of the following, the BEST title for the above passage is

    A. THE STENOGRAPHER AS DATA PROCESSOR
    B. THE RELATION OF KEYPUNCHING TO STENOGRAPHY
    C. UNDERSTANDING DATA PROCESSING
    D. PERMANENT OFFICE RECORDS

1.____

2. According to the above passage, a stenographer should understand the basic operations of data processing because

    A. almost every office today has contact with data processed by computer
    B. any office worker may be asked to verify the accuracy of data
    C. most offices are involved in the production of permanent records
    D. data may be converted into computer language by typing on a keypunch

2.____

3. According to the above passage, the data which the computer understands is MOST often expressed as

    A. a scientific programming language
    B. records or symbols punched on tape, cards, or other mediums
    C. records on cards
    D. records on tape

3.____

4. According to the above passage, computers are used MOST often to handle

    A. management data
    B. problems of higher education
    C. the control of chemical processes
    D. payroll operations

4._

5. Computer programming is taught in many colleges and business schools. The above passage implies that programmers in industry

    A. must have professional training
    B. need professional training to advance
    C. must have at least a college education to do adequate programming tasks
    D. do not need college education to do programming work

5._

6. According to the above passage, data to be processed by computer should be

    A. recent   B. basic
    C. complete   D. verified

6._

Questions 7-10.

DIRECTIONS: Questions 7 through 10 are to be answered SOLELY on the basis of the following passage.

There is nothing that will take the place of good sense on the part of the stenographer. You may be perfect in transcribing exactly what the dictator says and your speed may be adequate, but without an understanding of the dictator's intent as well as his words, you are likely to be a mediocre secretary.

A serious error that is made when taking dictation is putting down something that does not make sense. Most people who dictate material would rather be asked to repeat and explain than to receive transcribed material which has errors due to inattention or doubt. Many dictators request that their grammar be corrected by their secretaries, but unless specifically asked to do so, secretaries should not do it without first checking with the dictator. Secretaries should be aware that, in some cases, dictators may use incorrect grammar or slang expressions to create a particular effect.

Some people dictate commas, periods, and paragraphs, while others expect the stenographer to know when, where, and how to punctuate. A well-trained secretary should be able to indicate the proper punctuation by listening to the pauses and tones of the dictator's voice.

A stenographer who has taken dictation from the same person for a period of time should be able to understand him under most conditions, By increasing her tact, alertness, and efficiency, a secretary can become more competent.

7. According to the above passage, which of the following statements concerning the dictation of punctuation is CORRECT?

    A. Dictator may use incorrect punctuation to create a desired style
    B. Dictator should indicate all punctuation
    C. Stenographer should know how to punctuate based on the pauses and tones of the dictator
    D. Stenographer should not type any punctuation if it has not been dictated to her

7._

8. According to the above passage, how should secretaries handle grammatical errors in a   8.____
   dictation? Secretaries should

   A. *not correct* grammatical errors unless the dictator is aware that this is being done
   B. *correct* grammatical errors by having the dictator repeat the line with proper
      pauses
   C. *correct* grammatical errors if they have checked the correctness in a grammar book
   D. *correct* grammatical errors based on their own good sense

9. If a stenographer is confused about the method of spacing and indenting of a report   9.____
   which has just been dictated to her, she GENERALLY should

   A. do the best she can
   B. ask the dictator to explain what she should do
   C. try to improve her ability to understand dictated material
   D. accept the fact that her stenographic ability is not adequate

10. In the last line of the first paragraph, the word *mediocre* means MOST NEARLY   10.____

    A. superior   B. respected
    C. disregarded   D. second-rate

Questions 11-12.

DIRECTIONS: Questions 11 and 12 are to be answered SOLELY on the basis of the following
              passage.

The number of legible carbon copies required to be produced determines the weight of
the carbon paper to be used. When only one copy is made, heavy carbon paper is satisfactory. Most typists, however, use medium-weight carbon paper and find it serviceable for up to
three or four copies. If five or more copies are to be made, it is wise to use light carbon paper.
On the other hand, the finish of carbon paper to be used depends largely on the stroke of the
typist and, in lesser degree, on the number of copies to be made and on whether the typewriter has pica or elite type. A soft-finish carbon paper should be used if the typist's touch is
light or if a noiseless machine is used. It is desirable for the average typist to use medium-fin-
ish carbon paper for ordinary work, when only a few carbon copies are required. Elite type
requires a harder carbon finish than pica type for the same number of copies.

11. According to the above passage, the lighter the carbon paper used,   11.____

    A. the softer the finish of the carbon paper will be
    B. the greater the number of legible carbon copies that can be made
    C. the greater the number of times the carbon paper can be used
    D. the lighter the typist's touch should be

12. According to the above passage, the MOST important factor which determines whether   12.____
    the finish of carbon paper to be used in typing should be hard, medium, or soft is

    A. the touch of the typist
    B. the number of carbon copies required
    C. whether the type in the typewriter is pica or elite
    D. whether a machine with pica type will produce the same number of carbon copies
       as a machine with elite type

Questions 13-16.

DIRECTIONS: Questions 13 through 16 are to be answered SOLELY on the basis of the following passage.

Modern office methods, geared to ever higher speeds and aimed at ever greater efficiency, are largely the result of the typewriter. The typewriter is a substitute for handwriting
and, in the hands of a skilled typist, not only turns out letters and other documents at least
three times faster than a penman can do the work, but turns out the greater volume more uni-
formly and legibly. With the use of carbon paper and onionskin paper, identical copies can be
made at the same time.

The typewriter, besides its effect on the conduct of business and government, has had a
very important effect on the position of women. The typewriter has done much to bring
women into business and government, and today there are vastly more women than men typists. Many women have used the keys of the typewriter to climb the ladder to responsible
managerial positions.

The typewriter, as its name implies, employs type to make an ink impression on paper.
For many years, the manual typewriter was the standard machine used. Today, the electric
typewriter is dominant, and completely automatic electronic typewriters are coming into wider
use.

The mechanism of the office manual typewriter includes a set of keys arranged system-
atically in rows; a semicircular frame of type, connected to the keys by levers; the carriage, or
paper carrier; a rubber roller, called a platen, against which the type strikes; and an inked ribbon which make the impression of the type character when the key strikes it.

13. The above passage mentions a number of good features of the combination of a skilled   13.___
typist and a typewriter. Of the following, the feature which is NOT mentioned in the passage is

   A. speed   B. reliability
   C. uniformity   D. legibility

14. According to the above passage, a skilled typist can   14.___

   A. turn out at least five carbon copies of typed matter
   B. type at least three times faster than a penman can write
   C. type more than 80 words a minute
   D. readily move into a managerial position

15. According to the above passage, which of the following is NOT part of the mechanism of   15.___
a manual typewriter?

   A. Carbon paper   B. Platen
   C. Paper carrier   D. Inked ribbon

16. According to the above passage, the typewriter has helped   16.___

   A. men more than women in business
   B. women in career advancement into management
   C. men and women equally, but women have taken better advantage of it
   D. more women than men, because men generally dislike routine typing work

Questions 17-21.

DIRECTIONS: Questions 17 through 21 are to be answered SOLELY on the basis of the following passage.

The recipient gains an impression of a typewritten letter before he begins to read the
message. Factors which provide for a good first impression include margins and spacing that
are visually pleasing, formal parts of the letter which are correctly placed according to the
style of the letter, copy which is free of obvious erasures and over-strikes, and transcript that
is even and clear. The problem for the typist is that of how to produce that first, positive
impression of her work.

There are several general rules which a typist can follow when she wishes to prepare a
properly spaced letter on a sheet of letterhead. Ordinarily, the width of a letter should not be
less than four inches nor more than six inches. The side margins should also have a desirable
relation to the bottom margin and the space between the letterhead and the body of the letter.
Usually the most appealing arrangement is when the side margins are even and the bottom
margin is slightly wider than the side margins. In some offices, however, standard line length
is used for all business letters, and the secretary then varies the spacing between the date
line and the inside address according to the length of the letter.

17. The BEST title for the above passage would be   17.____

    A.   WRITING OFFICE LETTERS
    B.   MAKING GOOD FIRST IMPRESSIONS
    C.   JUDGING WELL-TYPED LETTERS
    D.   GOOD PLACING AND SPACING FOR OFFICE LETTERS

18. According to the above passage, which of the following might be considered the way in   18.____
which people very quickly judge the quality of work which has been typed? By

    A.   measuring the margins to see if they are correct
    B.   looking at the spacing and cleanliness of the typescript
    C.   scanning the body of the letter for meaning
    D.   reading the date line and address for errors

19. What, according to the above passage, would be definitely UNDESIRABLE as the aver-   19.____
age line length of a typed letter?

    A.   4"   B.   6"
    C.   5"   D.   7"

20. According to the above passage, when the line length is kept standard, the secretary   20.____

    A.   does not have to vary the spacing at all since this also is standard
    B.   adjusts the spacing between the date line and inside address for different lengths
of letters
    C.   uses the longest line as a guideline for spacing between the date line and inside
address
    D.   varies-the number of spaces between the lines

21. According to the above passage, side margins are MOST pleasing when they   21.__

     A.   are even and somewhat smaller than the bottom margin
     B.   are slightly wider than the bottom margin
     C.   vary with the length of the letter
     D.   are figured independently from the letterhead and the body of the letter

Questions 22-25.

DIRECTIONS: Questions 22 through 25 are to be answered SOLELY on the basis of the following passage.

Typed pages can reflect the simplicity of modern art in a machine age. Lightness and evenness can be achieved by proper layout and balance of typed lines and white space. Instead of solid, cramped masses of uneven, crowded typing, there should be a pleasing balance up and down as well as horizontal.

To have real balance, your page must have a center. The eyes see the center of the sheet slightly above the real center. This is the way both you and the reader see it. Try imagining a line down the center of the page that divides the paper in equal halves. On either side of your paper, white space and blocks of typing need to be similar in size and shape. Although left and right margins should be equal, top and bottom margins need not be as exact. It looks better to hold a bottom border wider than a top margin, so that your typing rests upon a cushion of white space. To add interest to the appearance of the page, try making one paragraph between one-half and two-thirds the size of an adjacent paragraph.

Thus, by taking full advantage of your typewriter, the pages that you type will not only be accurate but will also be attractive.

22. It can be inferred from the above passage that the basic importance of proper balancing   22.__
    on a typed page is that proper balancing

     A.   makes a typed page a work of modern art
     B.   provides exercise in proper positioning of a typewriter
     C.   increases the amount of typed copy on the paper
     D.   draws greater attention and interest to the page

23. A reader will tend to see the center of a typed page   23.__

     A.   somewhat higher than the true center
     B.   somewhat lower than the true center
     C.   on either side of the true center
     D.   about two-thirds of an inch above the true center

24. Which of the following suggestions is NOT given by the above passage?   24.__

     A.   Bottom margins may be wider than top borders.
     B.   Keep all paragraphs approximately the same size.
     C.   Divide your page with an imaginary line down the middle.
     D.   Side margins should be equalized.

25. Of the following, the BEST title for the above passage is   25._____

    A. INCREASING THE ACCURACY OF THE TYPED PAGE
    B. DETERMINATION OF MARGINS FOR TYPED COPY
    C. LAYOUT AND BALANCE OF THE TYPED PAGE
    D. HOW TO TAKE FULL ADVANTAGE OF THE TYPEWRITER

KEY (CORRECT ANSWERS)

1. C		11. B
2. A		12. A
3. B		13. C
4. A		14. B
5. D		15. A
6. D		16. B
7. C		17. D
8. A		18. B
9. B		19. D
10. D		20. B

21. A
22. D
23. A
24. B
25. C

TEST 3

DIRECTIONS: Each question or incomplete statement is followed by several suggested answers or completions. Select the one that BEST answers the question or completes the statement. *PRINT THE LETTER OF THE CORRECT ANSWER IN THE SPACE AT THE RIGHT.*

Questions 1-5.

DIRECTIONS: Questions 1 through 5 are to be answered SOLELY on the basis of the following passage.

A written report is a communication of information from one person to another. It is an account of some matter especially investigated, however routine that matter may be. The ultimate basis of any good written report is facts, which become known through observation and verification. Good written reports may seem to be no more than general ideas and opinions. However, in such cases, the facts leading to these opinions were gathered, verified, and reported earlier, and the opinions are dependent upon these facts. Good style, proper form, and emphasis cannot make a good written report out of unreliable information and bad judgment; but on the other hand, solid investigation and brilliant thinking are not likely to become very useful until they are effectively communicated to others. If a person's work calls for written reports, then his work is often no better than his written reports.

1. Based on the information in the above passage, it can be concluded that opinions expressed in a report should be

   A. based on facts which are gathered and reported
   B. emphasized repeatedly when they result from a special investigation
   C. kept to a minimum
   D. separated from the body of the report

1 ___

2. In the above passage, the one of the following which is mentioned as a way of establishing facts is

   A. authority   B. reporting
   C. communication   D. verification

2 ___

3. According to the above passage, the characteristic shared by ALL written reports is that they are

   A. accounts of routine matters   B. transmissions of information
   C. reliable and logical   D. written in proper form

3 ___

4. Which of the following conclusions can logically be drawn from the information given in the above passage?

   A. Brilliant thinking can make up for unreliable information in a report.
   B. One method of judging an individual's work is the quality of the written reports he is required to submit.
   C. Proper form and emphasis can make a good report out of unreliable information.
   D. Good written reports that seem to be no more than general ideas should be rewritten.

4 ___

5. Which of the following suggested titles would be MOST appropriate for the above pas-   5.___
   sage?

      A. GATHERING AND ORGANIZING FACTS
      B. TECHNIQUES OF OBSERVATION
      C. NATURE AND PURPOSE OF REPORTS
      D. REPORTS AND OPINIONS: DIFFERENCES AND SIMILARITIES

Questions 6-8.

DIRECTIONS: Questions 6 through 8 are to be answered SOLELY on the basis of the follow-
              ing passage.

The most important unit of the mimeograph machine is a perforated metal drum over
which is stretched a cloth ink pad. A reservoir inside the drum contains the ink which flows
through the perforations and saturates the ink pad. To operate the machine, the operator first
removes from the machine the protective sheet, which keeps the ink from drying while the
machine is not in use. He then hooks the stencil face down on the drum, draws the stencil
smoothly over the drum, and fastens the stencil at the bottom. The speed with which the
drum turns determines the blackness of the copies printed. Slow turning gives heavy, black
copies; fast turning gives light, clear-cut reproductions. If reproductions are run on other than
porous paper, slip-sheeting is necessary to prevent smearing. Often, the printed copy fails to
drop readily as it comes from the machine. This may be due to static electricity. To remedy
this difficulty, the operator fastens a strip of tinsel from side to side near the impression roller
so that the printed copy just touches the soft stems of the tinsel as it is ejected from the
machine, thus grounding the static electricity to the frame of the machine.

6. According to the above passage,   6.___

      A. turning the drum fast produces light copies
      B. stencils should be placed face up on the drum
      C. ink pads should be changed daily
      D. slip-sheeting is necessary when porous paper is being used

7. According to the above passage, when a mimeograph machine is not in use,   7.___

      A. the ink should be drained from the drum
      B. the ink pad should be removed
      C. the machine should be covered with a protective sheet
      D. the counter should be set at zero

8. According to the above passage, static electricity is grounded to the frame of the mimeo- 8.___
   graph machine by means of

      A. a slip-sheeting device
      B. a strip of tinsel
      C. an impression roller
      D. hooks located at the top of the drum

Questions 9-10.

DIRECTIONS: Questions 9 and 10 are to be answered SOLELY on the basis of the following passage.

The proofreading of material typed from copy is performed more accurately and more speedily when two persons perform this work as a team. The person who did not do the typing should read aloud the original copy while the person who did the typing should check the reading against the typed copy. The reader should speak very slowly and repeat the figures, using a different grouping of numbers when repeating the figures. For example, in reading 1967, the reader may say *one-nine-six-seven* on first reading the figure and *nineteen-sixty-seven* on repeating the figure. The reader should read all punctuation marks, taking nothing for granted. Since mistakes can occur anywhere, everything typed should be proofread. To avoid confusion, the proofreading team should use the standard proofreading marks, which are given in most dictionaries.

9.   According to the above passage, the   9.__

    A.   person who holds the typed copy is called the reader
    B.   two members of a proofreading team should take turns in reading the typed copy aloud
    C.   typed copy should be checked by the person who did the typing
    D.   person who did not do the typing should read aloud from the typed copy

10.   According to the above passage,   10.__

    A.   it is unnecessary to read the period at the end of a sentence
    B.   typographical errors should be noted on the original copy
    C.   each person should develop his own set of proofreading marks
    D.   figures should be read twice

Questions 11-16.

DIRECTIONS: Questions 11 through 16 are to be answered SOLELY on the basis of the above passage.

Basic to every office is the need for proper lighting. Inadequate lighting is a familiar cause of fatigue and serves to create a somewhat dismal atmosphere in the office. One requirement of proper lighting is that it be of an appropriate intensity. Intensity is measured in foot candles. According to the Illuminating Engineering Society of New York, for casual seeing tasks such as in reception rooms, inactive file rooms, and other service areas, it is recommended that the amount of light be 30 foot-candles. For ordinary seeing tasks such as reading, work in active file rooms, and in mailrooms, the recommended lighting is 100 foot-candles. For very difficult seeing tasks such as accounting, transcribing, and business machine use, the recommended lighting is 150 foot-candles.

Lighting intensity is only one requirement. Shadows and glare are to be avoided. For example, the larger the proportion of a ceiling filled with lighting units, the more glare-free and comfortable the lighting will be. Natural lighting from windows is not too dependable because on dark wintry days, windows yield little usable light, and on sunny summer afternoons, the glare from windows may be very distracting. Desks should not face the windows. Finally, the main lighting source ought to be overhead and to the left of the user,

11. According to the above passage, insufficient light in the office may cause   11.____

    A. glare   B. tiredness
    C. shadows   D. distraction

12. Based on the above passage, which of the following must be considered when planning   12.____
lighting arrangements? The

    A. amount of natural light present
    B. amount of work to be done
    C. level of difficulty of work to be done
    D. type of activity to be carried out

13. It can be inferred from the above passage that a well-coordinated lighting scheme is   13.____
LIKELY to result in

    A. greater employee productivity
    B. elimination of light reflection
    C. lower lighting cost
    D. more use of natural light

14. Of the following, the BEST title for the above passage is   14.____

    A. CHARACTERISTICS OF LIGHT
    B. LIGHT MEASUREMENT DEVICES
    C. FACTORS TO CONSIDER WHEN PLANNING LIGHTING SYSTEMS
    D. COMFORT VS. COST WHEN DEVISING LIGHTING ARRANGEMENTS

15. According to the above passage, a foot-candle is a measurement of the   15.____

    A. number of bulbs used
    B. strength of the light
    C. contrast between glare and shadow
    D. proportion of the ceiling filled with lighting units

16. According to the above passage, the number of foot-candles of light that would be   16.____
needed to copy figures onto a payroll is _____ foot-candles.

    A. less than 30   B. 100
    C. 30   D. 150

Questions 17-23.

DIRECTIONS: Questions 17 through 23 are to be answered SOLELY on the basis of the following passage, which is the Fee Schedule of a hypothetical college.

FEE SCHEDULE

A. A candidate for any baccalaureate degree is not required to pay tuition fees for undergraduate courses until he exceeds 128 credits, Candidates exceeding 128 credits in undergraduate courses are charged at the rate of $100 a credit for each credit of undergraduate course work in excess of 128. Candidates for a baccalaureate degree who are taking graduate courses must pay the same fee as any other student taking graduate courses

B. Non-degree students and college graduates are charged tuition fees for courses, whether undergraduate or graduate, at the rate of $180 a credit. For such students, there is an additional charge of $150 for each class hour per week in excess of the number of course credits. For example, if a three-credit course meets five hours a week, there is an additional charge for the extra two hours. Graduate courses are shown with a (G) before the course number.

C. All students are required to pay the laboratory fees indicated after the number of credits given for that course.

D. All students must pay a $250 general fee each semester.

E. Candidates for a baccalaureate degree are charged a $150 medical insurance fee for each semester. All other students are charged a $100 medical insurance fee each semester.

17. Miss Burton is not a candidate for a degree. She registers for the following courses in the spring semester: Economics 12, 4 hours a week, 3 credits; History (G) 23, 4 hours a week, 3 credits; English 1, 2 hours a week, 2 credits. The TOTAL amount in fees that Miss Burton must pay is 17._

   A. less than $2000   B. at least $2000 but less than $2100
   C. at least $2100 but less than $2200   D. $2200 or over

18. Miss Gray is not a candidate for a degree. She registers for the following courses in the fall semester: History 3, 3 hours a week, 3 credits; English 5, 3 hours a week, 2 credits; Physics 5, 6 hours a week, 3 credits, laboratory fee $ 60; Mathematics 7, 4 hours a week, 3 credits. The TOTAL amount in fees that Miss Gray must pay is 18._

   A. less than $3150   B. at least $3150 but less than $3250
   C. at least $3250 but less than $3350   D. $3350 or over

19. Mr. Wall is a candidate for the Bachelor of Arts degree and has completed 126 credits. He registers for the following courses in the spring semester, his final semester at college: French 4, 3 hours a week, 3 credits; Physics (G) 15, 6 hours a week, 3 credits, laboratory fee $80; History (G) 33, 4 hours a week, 3 credits. The TOTAL amount in fees that this candidate must pay is 19._

   A. less than $2100   B. at least $2100 but less than $2300
   C. at least $2300 but less than $2500   D. $2500

20. Mr. Tindall, a candidate for the B.A. degree, has completed 122 credits of undergraduate courses. He registers for the following courses in his final semester: English 31, 3 hours a week, 3 credits; Philosophy 12, 4 hours a week, 4 credits; Anthropology 15, 3 hours a week, 3 credits; Economics (G) 68, 3 hours a week, 3 credits. The TOTAL amount in fees that Mr. Tindall must pay in his final semester is 20._

   A. less than $1200   B. at least $1200 but less than $1400
   C. at least $1400 but less than $1600   D. $1600

21. Mr. Cantrell, who was graduated from the college a year ago, registers for graduate courses in the fall semester. Each course for which he registers carries the same number of credits as the number of hours a week it meets.
If he pays a total of $1530; including a $100 laboratory fee, the number of credits for which he is registered is

    A. 4   B. 5   C. 6   D. 7

21.____

22. Miss Jayson, who is not a candidate for a degree, has, registered for several courses including a lecture course in History. She withdraws from the course in History for which she had paid the required course fee of $690. The number of hours that this course is scheduled to meet is

    A. 4   B. 5   C. 2   D. 3

22.____

23. Mr. Van Arsdale, a graduate of a college is Iowa, registers for the following courses in one semester: Chemistry 35, 5 hours a week, 3 credits; Biology 13, 4 hours a week, 3 credits, laboratory fee $150; Mathematics (G) 179, 3 hours a week, 3 credits.
The TOTAL amount in fees that Mr. Van Arsdale must pay is

    A. less than $2400
    B. at least $2400 but less than $2500
    C. at least $2500 but less than $2600
    D. at least $2600 or over

23.____

Questions 24-25.

DIRECTIONS: Questions 24 and 25 are to be answered SOLELY on the basis of the following passage.

A duplex envelope is an envelope composed of two sections securely fastened together so that they become one mailing piece. This type of envelope makes it possible for a first class letter to be delivered simultaneously with third or fourth class matter and yet not require payment of the much higher first class postage rate on the entire mailing. First class postage is paid only on the letter which goes in the small compartment, third or fourth class postage being paid on the contents of the larger compartment. The larger compartment generally has an ungummed flap or clasp for sealing. The first class or smaller compartment has a gummed flap for sealing. Postal regulations require that the exact amount of postage applicable to each compartment be separately attached to it.

24. On the basis of the above passage, it is MOST accurate to state that

    A. the smaller compartment is placed inside the larger compartment before mailing
    B. the two compartments may be detached and mailed separately
    C. two classes of mailing matter may be mailed as a unit at two different postage rates
    D. the more expensive postage rate is paid on the matter in the larger compartment

24.____

25. When a duplex envelope is used, the   25.___

    A. first class compartment may be sealed with a clasp
    B. correct amount of postage must be placed on each compartment
    C. compartment containing third or fourth class mail requires a gummed flap for sealing
    D. full amount of postage for both compartments may be placed on the larger compartment

———

KEY (CORRECT ANSWERS)

1.	A	11.	C
2.	D	12.	D
3.	B	13.	A
4.	B	14.	C
5.	C	15.	B
6.	A	16.	D
7.	C	17.	B
8.	B	18.	A
9.	C	19.	B
10.	D	20.	B

21.	C
22.	A
23.	C
24.	C
25.	B

———

BASIC FUNDAMENTALS OF FILING SCIENCE

I. COMMENTARY

    Filing is the systematic arrangement and storage of papers, cards, forms, catalogues, etc., so that they may be found easily and quickly. The importance of an efficient filing system cannot be emphasized too strongly. The filed materials form records which may be needed quickly to settle questions that may cause embarrassing situations if such evidence is not available. In addition to keeping papers in order so that they are readily available, the filing system must also be designed to keep papers in good condition. A filing system must be planned so that papers may be filed easily, withdrawn easily, and as quickly returned to their proper place. The cost of a filing system is also an important factor.

    The need for a filing system arose when the business man began to carry on negotiations on a large scale. He could no longer be intimate with the details of his business. What was needed in the early era was a spindle or pigeon-hole desk. Filing in pigeon-hole desks is now almost completely extinct. It was an unsatisfactory practice since pigeon holes were not labeled, and the desk was an untidy mess.

II. BASIS OF FILING

    The science of filing is an exact one and entails a thorough understanding of basic facts, materials, and methods. An overview of this important information now follows.

1. Types of files

    (1) SHANNON FILE

    This consists of a board, at one end of which are fastened two arches which may be opened laterally.

    (2) SPINDLE FILE

    This consists of a metal or wood base to which is attached a long, pointed spike. Papers are pushed down on the spike as received. This file is useful for temporary retention of papers.

    (3) BOX FILE

    This is a heavy cardboard or metal box, opening from the side like a book.

    (4) FLAT FILE

    This consists of a series of shallow drawers or trays, arranged like drawers in a cabinet.

    (5) BELLOWS FILE

    This is a heavy cardboard container with alphabetized or compartment sections, the ends of which are closed in such a manner that they resemble an accordion.

    (6) VERTICAL FILE

    This consists of one or more drawers in which the papers are stood on edge, usually in folders, and are indexed by guides. A series of two or more drawers in one unit is the usual file cabinet.

    (7) CLIP FILE

    This file has a large clip attached to a board and is very similar to the *SHANNON FILE.*

    (8) VISIBLE FILE

    Cards are filed flat in an overlapping arrangement which leaves a part of each card visible at all times.

    (9) ROTARY FILE

The *ROTARY FILE* has a number of visible card files attached to a post around which they can be revolved. The wheel file has visible cards which rotate around a horizontal axle.

   (10) TICKLER FILE

This consists of cards or folders marked with the days of the month, in which materials are filed and turned up on the appropriate day of the month.

2. Aids in filing

   (1) GUIDES

Guides are heavy cardboard, pasteboard, or bristol-board sheets the same size as folders. At the top is a tab on which is marked or printed the distinguishing letter, words, or numbers indicating the material filed in a section of the drawer.

   (2) SORTING TRAYS

Sorting trays are equipped with alphabetical guides to facilitate the sorting of papers preparatory to placing them in a file.

   (3) CODING

Once the classification or indexing caption has been determined, it must be indicated on the letter for filing purposes.

   (4) CROSS REFERENCE

Some letters or papers might easily be called for under two or more captions. For this purpose, a cross-reference card or sheet is placed in the folder or in the index.

3. Variations of filing systems

   (1) VARIADEX ALPHABETIC INDEX

Provides for more effective expansion of the alphabetic system.

   (2) TRIPLE-CHECK NUMERIC FILING

Entails a multiple cross-reference, as the name implies.

   (3) VARIADEX FILING

Makes use of color as an aid in filing.

   (4) DEWEY DECIMAL SYSTEM

The system is a numeric one used in libraries or for filing library materials in an office. This special type of filing system is used where material is grouped in finely divided categories, such as in libraries. With this method, all material to be filed is divided into ten major groups, from 000 to 900, and then subdivided into tens, units, and decimals.

4. Centralized filing

Centralized filing means keeping the files in one specific or central location. Decentralized filing means putting away papers in files of individual departments. The first step in the organization of a central filing department is to make a careful canvass of all desks in the offices. In this manner we can determine just what material needs to be filed, and what information each desk occupant requires from the central file. Only papers which may be used at some time by persons in the various offices should be placed in the central file. A paper that is to be used at some time by persons in the various offices should be placed in the central file. A paper that is to be used by one department only should never be filed in the central file.

5. Methods of filing

While there are various methods used for filing, actually there are only five basic systems: alphabetical, subject, numerical, geographic, and chronological. All other systems are derived from one of these or from a combination of two or more of them.

Since the purpose of a filing system is to store business records <u>systemically</u> so that any particular record can be found almost instantly when required, filing requires, in addition to the proper kinds of equipment and supplies, an effective method of indexing.

There are five basic systems of filing:

(1) ALPHABETIC FILING

Most filing is alphabetical. Other methods, as described below, require extensive alphabetization.

In alphabetic filing, lettered dividers or guides are arranged in alphabetic sequence. Material to be filed is placed behind the proper guide. All materials under each letter are also arranged alphabetically. Folders are used unless the file is a card index.

(2) SUBJECT FILING

This method is used when a single, complete file on a certain subject is desired. A subject file is often maintained to assemble all correspondence on a certain subject. Such files are valuable in connection with insurance claims, contract negotiations, personnel, and other investigations, special programs, and similar subjects.

(3) GEOGRAPHICAL FILE

Materials are filed according to location: states, cities, counties, or other subdivisions. Statistics and tax information are often filed in this manner.

(4) CHRONOLOGICAL FILE

Records are filed according to date. This method is used especially in "tickler" files that have guides numbered 1 to 31 for each day of the month. Each number indicates the day of the month when the filed item requires attention.

(5) NUMERICAL FILE

This method requires an alphabetic card index giving name and number. The card index is used to locate records numbered consecutively in the files according to date received or sequence in which issued, such as licenses, permits, etc.

6. <u>Indexing</u>

Determining the name or title under which an item is to be filed is known as <u>indexing</u>. For example, how would a letter from Robert E. Smith be filed? The name would be rearranged Smith,Robert E., so that the letter would be filed under the last name.

7. <u>Alphabetizing</u>

The arranging of names for filing is known as <u>alphabetizing</u>. For example, suppose you have four letters indexed under the names Johnson, Becker, Roe, and Stern. How should these letters be arranged in the files so that they may be found easily? You would arrange the four names alphabetically, thus, Becker, Johnson, Roe, and Stern.

III. RULES FOR INDEXING AND ALPHABETIZING

1. The names of persons are to be transposed. Write the surname first, then the given name, and, finally, the middle name or initial. Then arrange the various names according to the alphabetic order of letters throughout the entire name. If there is a title, consider that after the middle name or initial.

NAMES	*INDEXED AS*
Arthur L.Bright	Bright, Arthur L.
Arthur S.Bright	Bright, Arthur S.
P.E. Cole	Cole, P.E.

Dr. John C. Fox   Fox, John C. (Dr.)

2. If a surname includes the same letters of another surname, with one or more additional letters added to the end, the shorter surname is placed first regardless of the given name or the initial of the given name.

NAMES	INDEXED AS
Robert E. Brown	Brown, Robert E.
Gerald A. Browne	Browne, Gerald A.
William O. Brownell	Brownell, William O.

3. Firm names are alphabetized under the surnames. Words like the, an, a, of, and for, are not considered.

NAMES	INDEXED AS
Bank of America	Bank of America
Bank Discount Dept.	Bank Discount Dept.
The Cranford Press	Cranford Press, The
Nelson Dwyer & Co.	Dwyer, Nelson, & Co.
Sears, Roebuck & Co.	Sears, Roebuck & Co.
Montgomery Ward & Co.	Ward, Montgomery, & Co.

4. The order of filing is determined first of all by the first letter of the names to be filed. If the first letters are the same, the order is determined by the second letters, and so on. In the following pairs of names, the order is determined by the letters underlined:

Austen   Hayes   Hanson   Harvey   Heath   Green   Schwartz
Baker   Heath   Harper   Harwood   Heaton   Greene   Schwarz

5. When surnames are alike, those with initials only precede those with given names, unless the first initial comes alphabetically after the first letter of the name.

Gleason, S.   *but,*   Abbott, Mary
Gleason, S.W.   Abbott, W.B.
Gleason, Sidney

6. Hyphenated names are treated as if spelled without the hyphen.

Lloyd, Paul N.   Lloyd, Robert
Lloyd-Jones, James   Lloyd-Thomas, A.S.

7. Company names composed of single letters which are not used as abbreviations precede the other names beginning with the same letter.

B & S Garage   E Z Duplicator Co.
B X Cable Co.   Eagle Typewriter Co.
Babbitt, R.N.   Edison Company

8. The ampersand (&) and the apostrophe (') in firm names are disregarded in alphabetizing.

Nelson & Niller   M & C Amusement Corp.
Nelson, Walter J.   M C Art Assn.
Nelson's Bakery

9. Names beginning with Mac, Mc, or M' are usually placed in regular order as spelled. Some filing systems file separately names beginning with Mc.

MacDonald, R.J.   Mazza, Anthony
Macdonald, S.B.   McAdam, Wm.
Mace, Wm.   McAndrews, Jerry

10. Names beginning with St. are listed as if the name Saint were spelled in full. Numbered street names and all abbreviated names are treated as if spelled out in full.

Saginaw   Fifth Avenue Hotel   Hart Mfg. Co.
St. Louis   42nd Street Dress Shop   Hart, Martin
St. Peter's Rectory   Hart, Chas.   Hart, Thos.

Sandford	Hart, Charlotte	Hart, Thomas A.
Smith, Wm.	Hart, Jas.	Hart, Thos. R.
Smith, Willis	Hart, Janice	

11. Federal, state, or city departments of government should be placed alphabetically under the governmental branch controlling them.

    Illinois, State of -- Departments and Commissions
      Banking Dept.
      Employment Bureau
    United States Government Departments
      Commerce
      Defense
      State
      Treasury

12. Alphabetic order

Each word in a name is an indexing unit. Arrange the names in alphabetic order by comparing similar units in each name. Consider the second units only when the first units are identical. Consider the third units only when both the first and second units are identical.

13. Single surnames or initials

A surname, when used alone, precedes the same surname with a first name or initial. A surname with a first initial only precedes a surname with a complete first name. This rule is sometimes stated, "nothing comes before something."

14. Surname prefixes

A surname prefix is not a separate indexing unit, but it is considered part of the surname. These prefixes include: d', D', Da, de, De, Del, Des, Di, Du, Fitz., La, Le, Mc, Mac, 'c, O', St., Van, Van der, Von, Von der, and others. The prefixes M', Mac, and Mc are indexed and filed exactly as they are spelled.

15. Names of firms

Names of firms and institutions are indexed and filed exactly as they are written when they do not contain the complete name of an individual.

16. Names of firms containing complete individual names

When the firm or institution name includes the complete name of an individual, the units are transposed for indexing in the same way as the name of an individual.

17. Article "The"

When the article the occurs at the beginning of a name, it is placed at the end in parentheses but it is not moved. In both cases, it is not an indexing unit and is disregarded in filing.

18. Hyphenated names

Hyphenated firm names are considered as separate indexing units. Hyphenated surnames of individuals are considered as one indexing unit; this applies also to hyphenated names of individuals whose complete names are part of a firm name.

19. Abbreviations

Abbreviations are considered as though the name were written in full; however, single letters other than abbreviations are considered as separate indexing units.

20. Conjunctions, prepositions and firm endings

Conjunctions and prepositions, such as and, for, in, of, are disregarded in indexing and filing but are not omitted or their order changed when writing names on cards and folders. Firm endings, such as Ltd., Inc., Co., Son, Bros., Mfg., and Corp., are treated as a unit in indexing and filing and are considered as though spelled in full, such as Brothers and Incorporated.

21. One or two words

Names that may be spelled either as one or two words are indexed and filed as one word.

22. Compound geographic names

Compound geographic names are considered as separate indexing and filing units, except when the first part of the name is not an English word, such as the Los in Los Angeles.

23. Titles or degrees of individuals, whether preceding or following the name, are not considered in indexing or filing. They are placed in parentheses after the given name or initial. Terms that designate seniority, such as Jr., Sr., 2d, are also placed in parentheses and are considered for indexing and filing only when the names to be indexed are otherwise identical.

Exception A:

When the name of an individual consists of a title and one name only, such as Queen Elizabeth, it is not transposed and the title is considered for indexing and filing.

Exception B:

When a title or foreign article is the initial word of a firm or association name, it is considered for indexing and filing.

24. Possessives

When a word ends in apostrophe s, the s is not considered in indexing and filing. However, when a word ends in s apostrophe, because the s is part of the original word, it is considered. This rule is sometimes stated, "Consider everything up to the apostrophe. "

25. United States and foreign government names

Names pertaining to the federal government are indexed and filed under United States Government and then subdivided by title of the department, bureau, division, commission, or board. Names pertaining to foreign governments are indexed and filed under names of countries and then subdivided by title of the department, bureau, division, commission, or board. Phrases, such as department of, bureau of, division of, commission of, board of, when used in titles of governmental bodies, are placed in parentheses after the word they modify, but are disregarded in indexing and filing. Such phrases, however, are considered in indexing and filing nongovernmental names.

26. Other political subdivisions

Names pertaining to other political subdivisions, such as states, counties, cities, or towns, are indexed and filed under the name of the political subdivision and then subdivided by the title of the department, bureau, division, commission, or board.

27. Addresses

When the same name appears with different addresses, the names are indexed as usual and arranged alphabetically according to city or town. The State is considered only when there is duplication of both individual or company name and city name. If the same name is located at different addresses within the same city, then the names are arranged alphabetically by streets. If the same name is located at more than one address on the same street, then the names are arranged from the lower to the higher street number.

28. Numbers

Any number in a name is considered as though it were written in words, and it is indexed and filed as one unit.

29. **Bank names**

Because the names of many banking institutions are alike in several respects, as first National Bank, Second National Bank, etc., banks are indexed and filed first by city location, then by bank name, with the state location written in parentheses and considered only if necessary

30. **Married women**

The legal name of a married woman is the one used for filing purposes. Legally, a man's surname is the only part of a man's name a woman assumes when she marries. Her legal name, therefore, could be either:

(1) Her own first and middle names together with her husband's surname, or
(2) Her own first name and maiden surname, together with her husband's surname.

Mrs. is placed in parentheses at the end of the name. Her husband's first and middle names are given in parentheses below her legal name.

31. An alphabetically arranged list of names illustrating many difficult points of alphabetizing follows.

COLUMN I	COLUMN II
Abbot , W.B.	54th St. Tailor Shop
Abbott, Alice	Forstall, W.J.
Allen, Alexander B.	44th St. Garage
Allen, Alexander B., Inc.	M A Delivery Co.
Andersen, Hans	M & C Amusement Corp.
Andersen, Hans E.	M C Art Assn.
Andersen, Hans E., Jr.	MacAdam, Wm.
Anderson, Andrew Andrews,	Macaulay, James
George Brown Motor Co., Boston	MacAulay, Wilson
Brown Motor Co., Chicago	MacDonald, R.J.
Brown Motor Co., Philadelphia	Macdonald, S.B.
Brown Motor Co., San Francisco	Mace, Wm.
Dean, Anna	Mazza, Anthony
Dean, Anna F.	McAdam, Wm.
Dean, Anna Frances	McAndrews, Jerry
Dean & Co.	Meade & Clark Co.
Deane-Arnold Apartments	Meade, S.T.
Deane's Pharmacy	Meade, Solomon
Deans, Felix A.	Sackett Publishing Co.
Dean's Studio	Sacks, Robert
Deans, Wm.	St.Andrew Hotel
Deans & Williams	St.John, Homer W.
East Randolph	Saks, Isaac B.
East St.Louis	Stephens, Ira
Easton, Pa.	Stevens, Delevan
Eastport, Me.	Stevens, Delila

IV. **OFFICIAL EXAMINATION DIRECTIONS AND RULES**

To preclude the possibility of conflicting or varying methods of filing, explicit directions and express rules are given to the candidate before he answers the filing questions on an examination.

The most recent official directions and rules for the filing questions are given immediately hereafter.

OFFICIAL DIRECTIONS

Each of questions ... to ... consists of four(five)names. For each question, select the one of the four(five)names that should be first (second)(third)(last) if the four(five)names were arranged in alphabetical order in accordance with the rules for alphabetical filing given below. Read these rules carefully. Then, for each question, indicate in the correspondingly numbered row on the answer sheet the letter preceding the name that should be first(second)(third)(last) in alphabetical order.

OFFICIAL RULES FOR ALPHABETICAL FILING

<u>Names of Individuals</u>

1. The names of individuals are filed in strict alphabetical order, first according to the last name, then according to first name or initial, and, finally, according to middle name or initial. For example: William Jones precedes George Kirk and Arthur S. Blake precedes Charles M. Blake.
2. When the last names are identical, the one with an initial instead of a first name precedes the one "with a first name beginning with the same initial. For example: J.Green precedes Joseph Green.
3. When identical last names also have identical first names, the one without a middle name or initial precedes the one with a middle name or initial. For example:Robert Jackson precedes both Robert C.Jackson and Robert Chester Jackson.
4. When last names are identical and the first names are also identical, the one with a middle initial precedes the one with a middle name beginning with the same initial. For example: Peter A. Brown precedes Peter Alvin Brown.
5. Prefixes such as De, El, La, and Van are considered parts of the names they precede. For example:Wilfred DeWald precedes Alexander Duval.
6. Last names beginning with "Mac" or "Mc" are filed as spelled.
7. Abbreviated names are treated as if they were spelled out. For example: Jos. is filed as Joseph and Robt. is filed as Robert.
8. Titles and designations such as Dr. ,Mrs., Prof. are disregarded in filing.

<u>Names of Business Organizations</u>

1. The names of business organizations are filed exactly as written, except that an organization bearing the name of an individual is filed alphabetically according to the name of the individual in accordance with the rules for filing names of individuals given above. For example: Thomas Allison Machine Company precedes Northern Baking Company.
2. When numerals occur in a name, they are treated as if they were spelled out. For example: 6 stands for six and 4th stands for fourth.
3. When the following words occur in names, they are disregarded: the, of, and Sample: Choose the name that should be filed *third.*

    (A) Fred Town   (2)   (C) D. Town   (1)
    (B) Jack Towne (3)   (D) Jack S.Towne (4)

The numbers in parentheses indicate the proper alphabetical order in which these names should be filed. Since the name that should be filed <u>third</u> is Jack Towne, the answer is (B).

FILING

EXAMINATION SECTION
TEST 1

DIRECTIONS: Questions 1 through 8 each show in Column I names written on four cards (lettered w, x, y, z) which have to be filed. You are to choose the option (lettered A, B, C, or D) in Column II which *BEST* represents the proper order of filing according to the Rules for Alphabetic Filing, given before, and the sample question given below. Print the letter of the correct answer in the space at the right.

SAMPLE QUESTION

	Column I		Column II
w.	Jane Earl	A.	w, y, z, x
x.	James A. Earle	B.	y, w, z, x
y.	James Earl	C.	x, y, w, z
z.	J. Earle	D.	x, w, y, z

The correct way to file the cards is:

y.	James Earl
w.	Jane Earl
z.	J. Earle
x.	James A. Earle

The correct filing order is shown by the letters, y, w, z, x (in that sequence). Since, in Column II, B appears in front of the letters, y, w, z, x (in that sequence), B is the correct answer to the sample question.

Now answer the following questions using that same procedure.

		Column I		Column II	
1.	w.	James Rothschild	A.	x, z, w, y	1.____
	x.	Julius B. Rothchild	B.	x, w, z, y	
	y.	B. Rothstein	C.	z, y, w, x	
	z.	Brian Joel Rothenstein	D.	z, w, x, y	
2.	w.	George S. Wise	A.	w, y, z, x	2.____
	x.	S. G. Wise	B.	x, w, y, z	
	y.	Geo. Stuart Wise	C.	y, x, w, z	
	z.	Prof. Diana Wise	D.	z, w, y, x	
3.	w.	10th Street Bus Terminal	A.	x, z, w, y	3.____
	x.	Buckingham Travel Agency	B.	y, x, w, z	
	y.	The Buckingham Theater	C.	w, z, y, x	
	z.	Burt Tompkins Studio	D.	x, w, y, z	
4.	w.	National Council of American Importers	A.	w, y, x, z	4.____
			B.	x, z, w, y	
	x.	National Chain Co. of Providence	C.	z, x, w, y	
	y.	National Council on Alcoholism	D.	z, x, y, w	
	z.	National Chain Co.			

5.	w.	Dr. Herbert Alvary	A.	w, y, x, z	5.___
	x.	Mr. Victor Alvarado	B.	z, w, x, y	
	y.	Alvar Industries	C.	y, z, x, w	
	z.	V. Alvarado	D.	w, z, x, y	
6.	w.	Joan MacBride	A.	w, x, z, y	6.___
	x.	Wm. Mackey	B.	w, y, z, x	
	y.	Roslyn McKenzie	C.	w, z, x, y	
	z.	Winifred Mackey	D.	w, y, x, z	
7.	w.	3 Way Trucking Co.	A.	y, x, z, w	7.___
	x.	3rd Street Bakery	B.	y, z, w, x	
	y.	380 Realty Corp.	C.	x, y, z, w	
	z.	Three Lions Pub	D.	x, y, w, z	
8.	w.	Miss Rose Leonard	A.	z, w, x, y	8.___
	x.	Rev. Leonard Lucas	B.	w, z, y, x	
	y.	Sylvia Leonard Linen Shop	C.	w, x, z, y	
	z.	Rose S. Leonard	D.	z, w, y, x	

KEY (CORRECT ANSWERS)

1. A
2. D
3. B
4. D
5. C
6. A
7. C
8. B

TEST 2

DIRECTIONS: Questions 1 through 7 each show in Column I four names (lettered w, x, y, z) which have to be entered in an agency telephone directory. You are to choose the option (lettered A, B, C, or D) in Column II which *BEST* represents the proper order for entering them according to the Rules for Alphabetic Filing, given before, and the sample question given below.

SAMPLE QUESTION

	Column I		Column II
w.	Doris Jenkin	A.	w, y, z, x
x.	Donald F. Jenkins	B.	y, w, z, x
y.	Donald Jenkin	C.	x, y, w, z
z.	D. Jenkins	D.	x, w, y, z

The correct way to enter these names is:
  y.   Donald Jenkin
  w.   Doris Jenkin
  z.   D. Jenkins
  x.   Donald F. Jenkins

The correct order is shown by the letters y, w, z, x, in that sequence. Since, in Column II, B appears in front of the letters y, w, z, x, in that sequence, B is the correct answer to the sample question.

Now answer the following questions using the same procedure.

		Column I		Column II		
1.	w.	Lawrence Robertson	A.	x, y, w, z	1._____	
	x.	Jack L. Robinson	B.	w, z, x, y		
	y.	John Robinson	C.	z, w, x, y		
	z.	William B. Roberson	D.	z, w, y, x		
2.	w.	P. N. Figueredo	A.	y, x, z, w	2._____	
	x.	M. Alice Figueroa	B.	x, z, w, y		
	y.	Jose Figueredo	C.	x, w, z, y		
	z.	M. Alicia Figueroa	D.	y, w, x, z		
3.	w.	George Steven Keats	A.	y, x, w, z	3._____	
	x.	George S. Keats	B.	z, y, x, w		
	y.	G. Samuel Keats	C.	x, z, w, y		
	z.	Dr. Samuel Keats	D.	w, z, x, y		
4.	w.	V. Merchant	A.	w, x, y, z	4._____	
	x.	Dr. William Mercher	B.	w, y, z, x		
	y.	Prof. Victor Merchant	C.	z, y, w, x		
	z.	Dr. Walter Merchan	D.	z, w, y, x		
5.	w.	Brian McCoy	A.	z, x, y, w	5._____	
	x.	William Coyne	B.	y, w, z, x		
	y.	Mr. William MacCoyle	C.	x, z, y, w		
	z.	Dr. D. V. Coyne	D.	w, y, z, x		

6.
w.	Ms. M. Rosie Buchanan	A.	z, y, x, w	6.___
x.	Rosalyn M. Buchanan	B.	w, z, x, y	
y.	Rosie Maria Buchanan	C.	w, z, y, x	
z.	Rosa Marie Buchanan	D.	z, x, y, w	

7.
w.	Prof. Jonathan Praga	A.	w, z, y, x	7.___
x.	Dr. Joan Prager	B.	w, x, z, y	
y.	Alan VanPrague	C.	x, w, z, y	
z.	Alexander Prague	D.	x, w, y, z	

———

KEY (CORRECT ANSWERS)

1. C
2. D
3. A
4. D
5. A
6. B
7. B

———

TEST 3

DIRECTIONS: Questions 1 through 10 each show in Column I names written on four cards (lettered w, x, y, z) which have to be filed. You are to choose the option (lettered A, B, C, or D) in Column II which *BEST* represents the proper order of filing according to the rules and sample question given below. The cards are to be filed according to the Rules for Alphabetical Filing, given before, and the sample question given below.

SAMPLE QUESTION

	Column I		Column II
w.	Jane Earl	A.	w, y, z, x
x.	James A. Earle	B.	y, w, z, x
y.	James Earl	C.	x, y, w, z
z.	J. Earle	D.	x, w, y, z

The correct way to file the cards is:

y.	James Earl
w.	Jane Earl
z.	J. Earle
x.	James A. Earle

The correct filing order is shown by the letters y, w, z, x (in that order). Since, in Column II, B appears in front of the letters y, w, z, x (in that order), B is the correct answer to the sample question.

Now answer Questions 1 through 10 using the same procedure.

		Column I		Column II	
1.	w.	John Smith	A.	w, x, y, z	1._____
	x.	Joan Smythe	B.	y, z, x, w	
	y.	Gerald Schmidt	C.	y, z, w, x	
	z.	Gary Schmitt	D.	z, y, w, x	
2.	w.	A. Black	A.	w, x, y, z	2._____
	x.	Alan S. Black	B.	w, y, x, z	
	y.	Allan Black	C.	w, y, z, x	
	z.	Allen A. Black	D.	x, w, y, z	
3.	w.	Samuel Haynes	A.	w, x, y, z	3._____
	x.	Sam C. Haynes	B.	x, w, z, y	
	y.	David Haynes	C.	y, z, w, x	
	z.	Dave L. Haynes	D.	z, y, x, w	
4.	w.	Lisa B. McNeil	A.	x, y, w, z	4._____
	x.	Tom MacNeal	B.	x, z, y, w	
	y.	Lisa McNeil	C.	y, w, z, x	
	z.	Lorainne McNeal	D.	z, x, y, w	
5.	w.	Larry Richardson	A.	w, y, x, z	5._____
	x.	Leroy Richards	B.	y, x, z, w	
	y.	Larry S. Richards	C.	y, z, x, w	
	z.	Leroy C. Richards	D.	x, w, z, y	

6.
   w. Arlene Lane
   x. Arlene Cora Lane
   y. Arlene Clair Lane
   z. Arlene C. Lane

A. w, z, y, x
B. w, z, x, y
C. y, x, z, w
D. z, y, w, x

6.__

7.
   w. Betty Fish
   x. Prof. Ann Fish
   y. Norma Fisch
   z. Dr. Richard Fisch

A. w, x, z, y
B. x, w, y, z
C. y, z, x, w
D. z, y, w, x

7.__

8.
   w. Dr. Anthony David Lukak
   x. Mr. Steven Charles Lucas
   y. Mr. Anthony J. Lukak
   z. Prof. Steven C. Lucas

A. w, y, z, x
B. x, z, w, y
C. z, x, y, w
D. z, x, w, y

8.__

9.
   w. Martha Y. Lind
   x. Mary Beth Linden
   y. Martha W. Lind
   z. Mary Bertha Linden

A. w, y, z, x
B. w, y, x, z
C. y, w, z, x
D. y, w, x, z

9.__

10.
   w. Prof. Harry Michael MacPhelps
   x. Mr. Horace M. MacPherson
   y. Mr. Harold M. McPhelps
   z. Prof. Henry Martin MacPherson

A. w, z, x, y
B. w, y, z, x
C. z, x, w, y
D. x, z, y, w

10.__

KEY (CORRECT ANSWERS)

1.	C	6.	A
2.	A	7.	C
3.	D	8.	D
4.	B	9.	C
5.	B	10.	A

TEST 4

DIRECTIONS: Answer Questions 1 through 5 on the basis of the following information:

A certain shop keeps an informational card file on all suppliers and merchandise. On each card is the supplier's name, the contract number for the merchandise he supplies, and a delivery date for the merchandise. In this filing system, the supplier's name is filed alphabetically, the contract number for the merchandise is filed numerically, and the delivery date is filed chronologically.

In Questions 1 through 5 there are five notations numbered 1 through 5 shown in Column I. Each notation is made up of a supplier's name, a contract number, and a date which is to be filed according to the following rules:

   First: File in alphabetical order;
   Second: When two or more notations have the same supplier, file according to the contract number in numerical order beginning with the lowest number;
   Third: When two or more notations have the same supplier and contract number, file according to the date beginning with the earliest date.

In Column II the numbers 1 through 5 are arranged in four ways to show four different orders in which the merchandise information might
be filed. Pick th.e answer (A., B, C, or D) in Column II in which the notations are arranged according to the above filing rules.

SAMPLE QUESTION

	Column I			Column II
1.	Cluney (4865) 6/17/02		A.	2, 3, 4, 1, 5
2.	Roster (2466) 5/10/01		B.	2, 5, 1, 3, 4
3.	Altool (7114) 10/15/02		C.	3, 2, 1, 4, 5
4.	Cluney (5296) 12/18/01		D.	3, 5, 1, 4, 2
5.	Cluney (4865) 4/8/02			

The correct way to file the cards is:

3.	Altool (7114) 10/15/02
5.	Cluney (4865) 4/8/02
1.	Cluney (4865) 6/17/02
4.	Cluney (5276) 12/18/01
2.	Roster (2466) 5/10/01

Since the correct filing order is 3, 5, 1, 4, 2, the answer to the sample question is D. Now answer Questions 1 through 5.

		Column I				Column II	
1.	1.	warren	(96063)	3/30/03	A.	2, 4, 3, 5, 1	1.____
	2.	moore	(21237)	9/4/04	B.	2, 3, 5, 4, 1	
	3.	newman	(10050)	12/12/03	C.	4, 5, 2, 3, 1	
	4.	downs	(81251)	1/2/03	D.	4, 2, 3, 5, 1	
	5.	oliver	(60145)	6/30/04			

2. 1. Henry (40552) 7/6/04   A. 5, 4, 3, 1, 2   2.__
    2. Boyd (91251) 9/1/03   B. 2, 3, 4, 1, 5
    3. George (8196) 12/12/03   C. 2, 4, 3, 1, 5
    4. George (31096) 1/12/04   D. 5, 2, 3, 1, 4
    5. West (6109) 8/9/03

3. 1. Salba (4670) 9/7/03   A. 5, 3, 1, 2, 4   3.__
    2. Salba (51219) 3/1/03   B. 3, 1, 2, 4, 5
    3. Crete (81562) 7/1/04   C. 3, 5, 4, 2, 1
    4. Salba (51219) 1/11/04   D. 5, 3, 4, 2, 1
    5. Texi (31549) 1/25/03

4. 1. Crayone (87105) 6/10/04   A. 1, 2, 5, 3, 4   4.__
    2. Shamba (49210) 1/5/03   B. 1, 5, 2, 3, 4
    3. Valiant (3152) 5/1/04   C. 1, 5, 3, 4, 2
    4. Valiant (3152) 1/9/04   D. 1, 5, 2, 4, 3
    5. Poro (59613) 7/1/03

5. 1. Mackie (42169) 12/20/03 A. 3, 2, 1, 5, 4   5.__
    2. Lebo (5198) 9/12/02   B. 3, 2, 4, 5, 1
    3. Drummon (99631) 9/9/04   C. 3, 5, 2, 4, 1
    4. Lebo (15311) 1/25/02   D. 3, 5, 4, 2, 1
    5. Harvin (81765) 6/2/03

KEY (CORRECT ANSWERS)

1. D
2. B
3. B
4. D
5. C

TEST 5

DIRECTIONS: Each of Questions 1 through 8 represents five cards to be filed, numbered 1 through 5 in Column I. Each card is made up of the employee's name, the date of a work assignment, and the work assignment code number shown in parentheses. The cards are to be filed according to the following rules:

First: File in alphabetical order;

Second: When two or more cards have the same employee's name, file according to the assignment date beginning with the earliest date;

Third: When two or more cards have the same employee's name and the same date, file according to the work assignment number beginning with the lowest number.

Column II shows the cards arranged in four different orders. Pick the answer (A, B, C, or D) in Column II which shows the cards arranged correctly according to the above filing rules.

SAMPLE QUESTION

	Column I				Column II
1.	Cluney	4/8/02	(486503)	A.	2, 3, 4, 1, 5
2.	Roster	5/10/01	(246611)	B.	2, 5, 1, 3, 4
3.	Altool	10/15/02	(711433)	C.	3, 2, 1, 4, 5
4.	Cluney	12/18/02	(527610)	D.	3, 5, 1, 4, 2
5.	Cluney	4/8/02	(486500)		

The correct way to file the cards is:

3. Altool 10/15/02 (711433)
5. Cluney 4/8/02 (486500)
1. Cluney 4/8/02 (486503)
4. Cluney 12/18/02 (527610)
2. Roster 5/10/01 (246611)

The correct filing order is shown by the numbers in front of each name (3, 5, 1, 4, 2). The answer to the sample question is the letter in Column II in front of the numbers 3, 5, 1, 4, 2. This answer is D.

Now answer Questions 1 through 8 according to these rules.

		Column I				Column II	
1.	1.	Kohls	4/2/02	(125677)	A.	1, 2, 3, 4, 5	1.____
	2.	Keller	3/21/02	(129698)	B.	3, 2, 1, 4, 5	
	3.	Jackson	4/10/02	(213541)	C.	3, 1, 2, 4, 5	
	4.	Richards	1/9/03	(347236)	D.	5, 2, 1, 3, 4	
	5.	Richmond	12/11/01	(379321)			
2.	1.	Burroughs	5/27/02	(237896)	A.	1, 4, 3, 2, 5	2.____
	2.	Charlson	1/16/02	(114537)	B.	4, 1, 5, 3, 2	
	3.	Carlsen	12/2/02	(114377)	C.	1, 4, 3, 5, 2	
	4.	Burton	5/1/02	(227096)	D.	4, 1, 3, 5, 2	
	5.	Charlson	12/2/02	(114357)			

3.	A.	Ungerer	11/11/02	(537924)	A.	1, 5, 3, 2, 4	3.
	B.	Winters	1/10/02	(657834)	B.	5, 1, 3, 4, 2	
	C.	Ventura	12/1/02	(698694)	C.	3, 5, 1, 2, 4	
	D.	Winters	10/11/02	(675654)	D.	1, 5, 3, 4, 2	
	E.	Ungaro	1/10/02	(684325)			
4.	1.	Norton	3/12/03	(071605)	A.	1, 4, 2, 3, 5	4.
	2.	Morris	2/26/03	(068931)	B.	3, 5, 2, 4, 1	
	3.	Morse	5/12/03	(142358)	C.	2, 4, 3, 5, 1	
	4.	Morris	2/26/03	(068391)	D.	4, 2, 5, 3, 1	
	5.	Morse	2/26/03	(068391)			
5.	1.	Eger	4/19/02	(874129)	A.	3, 4, 1, 2, 5	5
	2.	Eihler	5/19/03	(875329)	B.	1, 4, 5, 2, 3	
	3.	Ehrlich	11/19/02	(874839)	C.	4, 1, 3, 2, 5	
	4.	Eger	4/19/02	(876129)	D.	1, 4, 3, 5, 2	
	5.	Eihler	5/19/02	(874239)			
6.	1.	Johnson	12/21/02	(786814)	A.	2, 4, 3, 5, 1	6
	2.	Johns	12/21/03	(801024)	B.	4, 2, 5, 3, 1	
	3.	Johnson	12/12/03	(762814)	C.	4, 5, 3, 1, 2 ·	
	4.	Jackson	12/12/03	(862934)	D.	5, 3, 1, 2, 4	
	5.	Johnson	12/12/03	(762184)			
7.	1.	Fuller	7/12/02	(598310)	A.	2, 1, 5, 4, 3	7
	2.	Fuller	7/2/02	(598301)	B.	1, 2, 4, 5, 3	
	3.	Fuller	7/22/02	(598410)	C.	1, 4, 5, 2, 3	
	4.	Fuller	7/17/03	(598710)	D.	2, 1, 3, 5, 4	
	5.	Fuller	7/17/03	(598701)			
8.	1.	Perrine	10/27/99	(637096)	A.	3, 4, 5, 1, 2	8
	2.	Perrone	11/14/02	(767609)	B.	3, 2, 5, 4, 1	
	3.	Perrault	10/15/98	(629706)	C.	5, 3, 4, 1, 2	
	4.	Perrine	10/17/02	(373656)	D.	4, 5, 1, 2, 3	
	5.	Perine	10/17/01	(376356)			

KEY (CORRECT ANSWERS)

TEST 6

DIRECTIONS: Each question or incomplete statement is followed by several suggested answers or completions. Select the one that *BEST* answers the question or completes the statement. *PRINT THE LETTER OF THE CORRECT ANSWER IN THE SPACE AT THE RIGHT.*

1. Which one of the following *BEST* describes the usual arrangement of a tickler file?   1.____

   A.   Alphabetical   B.   Chronological
   C.   Numerical   D.   Geographical

2. Which one of the following is the *LEAST* desirable filing practice?   2.____

   A.   Using staples to keep papers together
   B.   Filing all material without regard to date
   C.   Keeping a record of all materials removed from the files
   D.   Writing filing instructions on each paper prior to filing

3. The one of the following records which it would be *MOST* advisable to keep in alphabeti-   3.____
    cal order is a

   A.   continuous listing of phone messages, including time and caller, for your supervi-
        sor
   B.   listing of individuals currently employed by your agency in a particular title
   C.   record of purchases paid for by the petty cash fund
   D.   dated record of employees who have borrowed material from the files in your office

4. Tickler systems are used in many legal offices for scheduling and calendar control. Of   4.____
    the following, the *LEAST* common use of a tickler system is to

   A.   keep papers filed in such a way that they may easily be retrieved
   B.   arrange for the appearance of witnesses when they will be needed
   C.   remind lawyers when certain papers are due
   D.   arrange for the gathering of certain types of evidence

5. A type of file which permits the operator to remain seated while the file can be moved   5.____
    backward and forward as required is *BEST* termed a

   A.   lateral file   B.   movable file
   C.   reciprocating file   D.   rotary file

6. In which of the following cases would it be *MOST* desirable to have two cards for one   6.____
    individual in a single alphabetic file? The individual has

   A.   a hyphenated surname
   B.   two middle names
   C.   a first name with an unusual spelling
   D.   a compound first name

KEY (CORRECT ANSWERS)

1. B
2. B
3. B
4. A
5. C
6. A

RECORD KEEPING
EXAMINATION SECTION
TEST 1

DIRECTIONS: Each question or incomplete statement is followed by several suggested answers or completions. Select the one that BEST answers the question or completes the statement. *PRINT THE LETTER OF THE CORRECT ANSWER IN THE SPACE AT THE RIGHT.*

Questions 1-15.

DIRECTIONS: Questions 1 through 15 are to be answered on the basis of the following list of company names below. Arrange a file alphabetically, word-by-word, disregarding punctuation, conjunctions, and apostrophes. Then answer the questions.

    A Bee C Reading Materials
    ABCO Parts
    A Better Course for Test Preparation
    AAA Auto Parts Co.
    A-Z Auto Parts, Inc.
    Aabar Books
    Abbey, Joanne
    Boman-Sylvan Law Firm
    BMW Autowerks
    C Q Service Company
    Chappell-Murray, Inc.
    E&E Life Insurance
    Emcrisco
    Gigi Arts
    Gordon, Jon & Associates
    SOS Plumbing
    Schmidt, J.B. Co.

1. Which of these files should appear FIRST?   1.____

    A. ABCO Parts
    B. A Bee C Reading Materials
    C. A Better Course for Test Preparation
    D. AAA Auto Parts Co.

2. Which of these files should appear SECOND?   2.____

    A. A-Z Auto Parts, Inc.
    B. A Bee C Reading Materials
    C. A Better Course for Test Preparation
    D. AAA Auto Parts Co.

3. Which of these files should appear THIRD?   3.____

    A. ABCO Parts
    B. A Bee C Reading Materials
    C. Aabar Books
    D. AAA Auto Parts Co.

4. Which of these files should appear FOURTH?   4.___

    A. Aabar Books
    B. ABCO Parts
    C. Abbey, Joanne
    D. AAA Auto Parts Co.

5. Which of these files should appear LAST?   5.___

    A. Gordon, Jon & Associates
    B. Gigi Arts
    C. Schmidt, J.B. Co.
    D. SOS Plumbing

6. Which of these files should appear between A-Z Auto Parts, Inc. and Abbey, Joanne?   6.___

    A. A Bee C Reading Materials
    B. AAA Auto Parts Co.
    C. ABCO Parts
    D. A Better Course for Test Preparation

7. Which of these files should appear between ABCO Parts and Aabar Books?   7.___

    A. A Bee C Reading Materials
    B. Abbey, Joanne
    C. Aabar Books
    D. A-Z Auto Parts

8. Which of these files should appear between Abbey, Joanne and Boman-Sylvan Law   8.___
Firm?

    A. A Better Course for Test Preparation
    B. BMW Autowerks
    C. Chappell-Murray, Inc.
    D. Aabar Books

9. Which of these files should appear between Abbey, Joanne and C Q Service?   9.___

    A. A-Z Auto Parts,Inc.   B. BMW Autowerks
    C. Choices A and B   D. Chappell-Murray, Inc.

10. Which of these files should appear between C Q Service Company and Emcrisco?   10.___

    A. Chappell-Murray, Inc.   B. E&E Life Insurance
    C. Gigi Arts   D. Choices A and B

11. Which of these files should NOT appear between C Q Service Company and E&E Life   11.___
Insurance?

    A. Gordon, Jon & Associates
    B. Emcrisco
    C. Gigi Arts
    D. All of the above

12. Which of these files should appear between Chappell-Murray Inc., and Gigi Arts?   12.____

    A. CQ Service Inc. E&E Life Insurance, and Emcrisco
    B. Emcrisco, E&E Life Insurance, and Gordon, Jon & Associates
    C. E&E Life Insurance and Emcrisco
    D. Emcrisco and Gordon, Jon & Associates

13. Which of these files should appear between Gordon, Jon & Associates and SOS Plumbing?   13.____

    A. Gigi Arts   B. Schmidt, J.B. Co.
    C. Choices A and B   D. None of the above

14. Each of the choices lists the four files in their proper alphabetical order except   14.____

    A. E&E Life Insurance; Gigi Arts; Gordon, Jon & Associates; SOS Plumbing
    B. E&E Life Insurance; Emcrisco; Gigi Arts; SOS Plumbing
    C. Emcrisco; Gordon, Jon & Associates; SOS Plumbing; Schmidt, J.B. Co.
    D. Emcrisco; Gigi Arts; Gordon, Jon & Associates; SOS Plumbing

15. Which of the choices lists the four files in their proper alphabetical order?   15.____

    A. Gigi Arts; Gordon, Jon & Associates; SOS Plumbing; Schmidt, J.B. Co.
    B. Gordon, Jon & Associates; Gigi Arts; Schmidt, J.B. Co.; SOS Plumbing
    C. Gordon, Jon & Associates; Gigi Arts; SOS Plumbing; Schmidt, J.B. Co.
    D. Gigi Arts; Gordon, Jon & Associates; Schmidt, J.B. Co.; SOS Plumbing

16. The alphabetical filing order of two businesses with identical names is determined by the   16.____

    A. length of time each business has been operating
    B. addresses of the businesses
    C. last name of the company president
    D. none of the above

17. In an alphabetical filing system, if a business name includes a number, it should be   17.____

    A. disregarded
    B. considered a number and placed at the end of an alphabetical section
    C. treated as though it were written in words and alphabetized accordingly
    D. considered a number and placed at the beginning of an alphabetical section

18. If a business name includes a contraction (such as *don't* or *it's*), how should that word be treated in an alphabetical filing system?   18.____

    A. Divide the word into its separate parts and treat it as two words.
    B. Ignore the letters that come after the apostrophe.
    C. Ignore the word that contains the contraction.
    D. Ignore the apostrophe and consider all letters in the contraction.

19. In what order should the parts of an address be considered when using an alphabetical filing system?   19.____

    A. City or town; state; street name; house or building number
    B. State; city or town; street name; house or building number
    C. House or building number; street name; city or town; state
    D. Street name; city or town; state

20. A business record should be cross-referenced when a(n)   20.__

    A. organization is known by an abbreviated name
    B. business has a name change because of a sale, incorporation, or other reason
    C. business is known by a *coined* or common name which differs from a dictionary spelling
    D. all of the above

21. A geographical filing system is MOST effective when   21.__

    A. location is more important than name
    B. many names or titles sound alike
    C. dealing with companies who have offices all over the world
    D. filing personal and business files

Questions 22-25.

DIRECTIONS: Questions 22 through 25 are to be answered on the basis of the list of items below, which are to be filed geographically. Organize the items geographically and then answer the questions.

    1. University Press at Berkeley, U.S.
    2. Maria Sanchez, Mexico City, Mexico
    3. Great Expectations Ltd. in London, England
    4. Justice League, Cape Town, South Africa, Africa
    5. Crown Pearls Ltd. in London, England
    6. Joseph Prasad in London, England

22. Which of the following arrangements of the items is composed according to the policy of: 22.__
Continent, Country, City, Firm or Individual Name?

    A. 5, 3, 4, 6, 2, 1   B. 4, 5, 3, 6, 2, 1
    C. 1, 4, 5, 3, 6, 2   D. 4, 5, 3, 6, 1, 2

23. Which of the following files is arranged according to the policy of: *Continent, Country,* 23.__
City, Firm or Individual Name?

    A. South Africa. Africa. Cape Town. Justice League
    B. Mexico. Mexico City, Maria Sanchez
    C. North America. United States. Berkeley. University Press
    D. England. Europe. London. Prasad, Joseph

24. Which of the following arrangements of the items is composed according to the policy of: 24.__
Country, City, Firm or Individual Name?

    A. 5, 6, 3, 2, 4, 1   B. 1, 5, 6, 3, 2, 4
    C. 6, 5, 3, 2, 4, 1   D. 5, 3, 6, 2, 4, 1

25. Which of the following files is arranged according to a policy of: *Country, City, Firm or* 25.__
Individual Name?

    A. England. London. Crown Pearls Ltd.
    B. North America. United States. Berkeley. University Press
    C. Africa. Cape Town. Justice League
    D. Mexico City. Mexico. Maria Sanchez

26. Under which of the following circumstances would a phonetic filing system be MOST effective?　　　　26.____

    A. When the person in charge of filing can't spell very well
    B. With large files with names that sound alike
    C. With large files with names that are spelled alike
    D. All of the above

Questions 27-29.

DIRECTIONS: Questions 27 through 29 are to be answered on the basis of the following list of numerical files.
    1. 391-023-100
    2. 361-132-170
    3. 385-732-200
    4. 381-432-150
    5. 391-632-387
    6. 361-423-303
    7. 391-123-271

27. Which of the following arrangements of the files follows a consecutive-digit system?　　　　27.____

    A. 2, 3, 4, 1　　　　　　　　　B. 1, 5, 7, 3
    C. 2, 4, 3, 1　　　　　　　　　D. 3, 1, 5, 7

28. Which of the following arrangements follows a terminal-digit system?　　　　28.____

    A. 1, 7, 2, 4, 3　　　　　　　B. 2, 1, 4, 5, 7
    C. 7, 6, 5, 4, 3　　　　　　　D. 1, 4, 2, 3, 7

29. Which of the following lists follows a middle-digit system?　　　　29.____

    A. 1, 7, 2, 6, 4, 5, 3　　　　B. 1, 2, 7, 4, 6, 5, 3
    C. 7, 2, 1, 3, 5, 6, 4　　　　D. 7, 1, 2, 4, 6, 5, 3

Questions 30-31.

DIRECTIONS: Questions 30 and 31 are to be answered on the basis of the following information.
    1. Reconfirm Laura Bates appointment with James Caldecort on December 12 at 9:30 A.M.
    2. Laurence Kinder contact Julia Lucas on August 3 and set up a meeting for week of September 23 at 4 P.M.
    3. John Lutz contact Larry Waverly on August 3 and set up appointment for September 23 at 9:30 A.M.
    4. Call for tickets for Gerry Stanton August 21 for New Jersey on September 23, flight 143 at 4:43 P.M.

30. A chronological file for the above information would be

    A. 4, 3, 2, 1   B. 3, 2, 4, 1
    C. 4, 2, 3, 1   D. 3, 1, 2, 4

30.____

31. Using the above information, a chronological file for the date of September 23 would be

    A. 2, 3, 4   B. 3, 1, 4   C. 3, 2, 4   D. 4, 3, 2

31.____

Questions 32-34.

DIRECTIONS: Questions 32 through 34 are to be answered on the basis of the following information.
1. Call Roger Epstein, Ashoke Naipaul, Jon Anderson, and Sarah Washington on April 19 at 1:00 P.M. to set up meeting with Alika D'Ornay for June 6 in New York.
2. Call Martin Ames before noon on April 19 to confirm afternoon meeting with Bob Greenwood on April 20th
3. Set up meeting room at noon for 2:30 P.M. meeting on April 19th;
4. Ashley Stanton contact Bob Greenwood at 9:00 A.M. on April 20 and set up meeting for June 6 at 8:30 A.M.
5. Carol Guiland contact Shelby Van Ness during afternoon of April 20 and set up meeting for June 6 at 10:00 A.M.
6. Call airline and reserve tickets on June 6 for Roger Epstein trip *to* Denver on July 8
7. Meeting at 2:30 P.M. on April 19th

32. A chronological file for all of the above information would be

    A. 2, 1, 3, 7, 5, 4, 6   B. 3, 7, 2, 1, 4, 5, 6
    C. 3, 7, 1, 2, 5, 4, 6   D. 2, 3, 1, 7, 4, 5, 6

32.____

33. A chronological file for the date of April 19th would be

    A. 2, 3, 7, 1   B. 2, 3, 1, 7
    C. 7, 1, 3, 2   D. 3, 7, 1, 2

33.____

34. Add the following information to the file, and then create a chronological file for April 20th:
8. April 20: 3:00 P.M. meeting between Bob Greenwood and Martin Ames.

    A. 4, 5, 8   B. 4, 8, 5   C. 8, 5, 4   D. 5, 4, 8

34.____

35. The PRIMARY advantage of computer records filing over a manual system is

    A. speed of retrieval   B. accuracy
    C. cost   D. potential file loss

35.____

KEY (CORRECT ANSWERS)

1.	B		16.	B
2.	C		17.	C
3.	D		18.	D
4.	A		19.	A
5.	D		20.	D
6.	C		21.	A
7.	B		22.	B
8.	B		23.	C
9.	C		24.	D
10.	D		25.	A
11.	D		26.	B
12.	C		27.	C
13.	B		28.	D
14.	C		29.	A
15.	D		30.	B

31. C
32. D
33. B
34. A
35. A

———

PREPARING WRITTEN MATERIAL

PARAGRAPH REARRANGEMENT
COMMENTARY

The sentences which follow are in scrambled order. You are to rearrange them in proper order and indicate the letter choice containing the correct answer at the space at the right.

Each group of sentences in this section is actually a paragraph presented in scrambled order. Each sentence in the group has a place in that paragraph; no sentence is to be left out. You are to read each group of sentences and decide upon the best order in which to put the sentences so as to form as well-organized paragraph.

The questions in this section measure the ability to solve a problem when all the facts relevant to its solution are not given.

More specifically, certain positions of responsibility and authority require the employee to discover connections between events sometimes, apparently, unrelated. In order to do this, the employee will find it necessary to correctly infer that unspecified events have probably occurred or are likely to occur. This ability becomes especially important when action must be taken on incomplete information.

Accordingly, these questions require competitors to choose among several suggested alternatives, each of which presents a different sequential arrangement of the events. Competitors must choose the MOST logical of the suggested sequences.

In order to do so, they may be required to draw on general knowledge to infer missing concepts or events that are essential to sequencing the given events. Competitors should be careful to infer only what is essential to the sequence. The plausibility of the wrong alternatives will always require the inclusion of unlikely events or of additional chains of events which are NOT essential to sequencing the given events.

It's very important to remember that you are looking for the best of the four possible choices, and that the best choice of all may not even be one of the answers you're given to choose from.

There is no one right way to these problems. Many people have found it helpful to first write out the order of the sentences, as they would have arranged them, on their scrap paper before looking at the possible answers. If their optimum answer is there, this can save them some time. If it isn't, this method can still give insight into solving the problem. Others find it most helpful to just go through each of the possible choices, contrasting each as they go along. You should use whatever method feels comfortable, and works, for you.

While most of these types of questions are not that difficult, we've added a higher percentage of the difficult type, just to give you more practice. Usually there are only one or two questions on this section that contain such subtle distinctions that you're unable to answer confidently, and you then may find yourself stuck deciding between two possible choices, neither of which you're sure about.

———

EXAMINATION SECTION
TEST 1

DIRECTIONS: The following groups of sentences need to be arranged in an order that makes sense. Select the letter preceding the sequence that represents the BEST sentence order. *PRINT THE LETTER OF THE CORRECT ANSWER IN THE SPACE AT THE RIGHT.*

1.   I.   The keyboard was purposely designed to be a little awkward to slow typists down.   1.____
        II.   The arrangement of letters on the keyboard of a typewriter was not designed for the convenience of the typist.
        III.   Fortunately, no one is suggesting that a new keyboard be designed right away.
        IV.   If one were, we would have to learn to type all over again.
        V.   The reason was that the early machines were slower than the typists and would jam easily.

        A.   I, III, IV, II, V   B.   II, V, I, IV, III
        C.   V, I, II, III, IV   D.   II, I, V, III, IV

2.   I.   The majority of the new service jobs are part-time or low-paying.   2.____
        II.   According to the U.S. Bureau of Labor Statistics, jobs in the service sector constitute 72% of all jobs in this country.
        III.   If more and more workers receive less and less money, who will buy the goods and services needed to keep the economy going?
        IV.   The service sector is by far the fastest growing part of the United States economy.
        V.   Some economists look upon this trend with great concern.

        A.   II, IV, I, V, III   B.   II, III, IV, I, V
        C.   V, IV, II, III, I   D.   III, I, II, IV, V

3.   I.   They can also affect one's endurance.   3.____
        II.   This can stabilize blood sugar levels, and ensure that the brain is receiving a steady, constant supply of glucose, so that one is *hitting on all cylinders* while taking the test.
        III.   By food, we mean real food, not junk food or unhealthy snacks.
        IV.   For this reason, it is important not to skip a meal, and to bring food with you to the exam.
        V.   One's blood sugar levels can affect how clearly one is able to think and concentrate during an exam.

        A.   V, IV, II, III, I   B.   V, II, I, IV, III
        C.   V, I, IV, III, II   D.   V, IV, I, III, II

4.   I.   Those who are the embodiment of desire are absorbed in material quests, and those who are the embodiment of feeling are warriors who value power more than possession.   4.____
        II.   These qualities are in everyone, but in different degrees.
        III.   But those who value understanding yearn not for goods or victory, but for knowledge.
        IV.   According to Plato, human behavior flows from three main sources: desire, emotion, and knowledge,

V. In the perfect state, the industrial forces would produce but not rule, the military would protect but not rule, and the forces of knowledge, the philosopher kings, would reign.

A. IV, V, I, II, III	B. V, I, II, III, IV
C. IV, III, II, I, V	D. IV, II, I, III, V

5.　I. Of the more than 26,000 tons of garbage produced daily in New York City, 12,000 tons arrive daily at Fresh Kills.

II. In a month, enough garbage accumulates there to fill the Empire State Building.

III. In 1937, the Supreme Court halted the practice of dumping the trash of New York City into the sea.

IV. Although the garbage is compacted, in a few years the mounds of garbage at Fresh Kills will be the highest points south of Maine's Mount Desert Island on the Eastern Seaboard.

V. Instead, tugboats now pull barges of much of the trash to Staten Island and the largest landfill in the world, Fresh Kills.

5.____

A. III, V, IV, I, II	B. III, V, II, IV, I
C. III, V, I, II, IV	D. III, II, V, IV, I

6.　I. Communists rank equality very high, but freedom very low.

II. Unlike communists, conservatives place a high value on freedom and a very low value on equality.

III. A recent study demonstrated that one way to classify people's political beliefs is to look at the importance placed on two words: freedom and equality.

IV. Thus, by demonstrating how members of these groups feel about the two words, the study has proved to be useful for political analysts in several European countries.

V. According to the study, socialists and liberals rank both freedom and equality very high, while fascists rate both very low.

6.____

A. III, V, I, II, IV	B. III, IV, V, I, II
C. III, V, IV, II, I	D. III, I, II, IV, V

7.　I. "Can there be anything more amazing than this?"

II. If the riddle is successfully answered, his dead brothers will be brought back to life.

III. "Even though man sees those around him dying every day," says Dharmaraj, "he still believes and acts as if he were immortal."

IV. "What is the cause of ceaseless wonder?" asks the Lord of the Lake.

V. In the ancient epic, The Mahabharata, a riddle is asked of one of the Pandava brothers.

7.____

A. V, II, I, IV, III	B. V, IV, III, I, II
C. V, II, IV, III, I	D. V, II, IV, I, III

8.   I.   On the contrary, the two main theories — the cooperative (neoclassical) theory and   8.____
the radical (labor theory) — clearly rest on very different assumptions, which have
very different ethical overtones.

       II.   The distribution of income is the primary factor in determining the relative levels
of material well-being that different groups or individuals attain.

      III.   Of all issues in economics, the distribution of income is one of the most contro-
versial.

      IV.   The neoclassical theory tends to support the existing income distribution (or
minor changes), while the labor theory tends to support substantial changes in
the way income is distributed.

       V.   The intensity of the controversy reflects the fact that different economic theories
are not purely neutral, *detached* theories with no ethical or moral implications.

    A. II, I, V, IV, III   B. III, II, V, I, IV
    C. III, V, II, I, IV   D. III, V, IV, I, II

9.   I.   The pool acts as a broker and ensures that the cheapest power gets used first.   9.____

       II.   Every six seconds, the pool's computer monitors all of the generating stations in
the state and decides which to ask for more power and which to cut back.

      III.   The buying and selling of electrical power is handled by the New York Power
Pool in Guilderland, New York.

      IV.   This is to the advantage of both the buying and selling utilities.

       V.   The pool began operation in 1970, and consists of the state's eight electric utili-
ties.

    A. V, I, II, III, IV   B. IV, II, I, III, V
    C. III, V, I, IV, II   D. V, III, IV, II, I

10.   I.   Modern English is much simpler grammatically than Old English.   10.____

       II.   Finnish grammar is very complicated; there are some fifteen cases, for example.

      III.   Chinese, a very old language, may seem to be the exception, but it is the great
number of characters/ words that must be mastered that makes it so

      IV.   difficult to learn, not its grammar.

       V.   The newest literary language — that is, written as well as spoken — is Finnish,
whose literary roots go back only to about the middle of the nineteenth century.

      VI.   Contrary to popular belief, the longer a language is been in use the simpler its
grammar — not the reverse.

    A. IV, I, II, III, V   B. V, I, IV, II, III
    C. I, II, IV, III, V   D. IV, II, III, I, V

KEY (CORRECT ANSWERS)

1.	D	6.	A
2.	A	7.	C
3.	C	8.	B
4.	D	9.	C
5.	C	10.	B

TEST 2

DIRECTIONS: This type of question tests your ability to recognize accurate paraphrasing, well-constructed paragraphs, and appropriate style and tone. It is important that the answer you select contains only the facts or concepts given in the original sentences. It is also important that you be aware of incomplete sentences, inappropriate transitions, unsupported opinions, incorrect usage, and illogical sentence order. Paragraphs that do not include all the necessary facts and concepts, that distort them, or that add new ones are not considered correct.

The format for this section may vary. Sometimes, long paragraphs are given, and emphasis is placed on style and organization. Our first five questions are of this type. Other times, the paragraphs are shorter, and there is less emphasis on style and more emphasis on accurate representation of information. Our second group of five questions are of this nature.

For each of Questions 1 through 10, select the paragraph that BEST expresses the ideas contained in the sentences above it. *PRINT THE LETTER OF THE CORRECT ANSWER IN THE SPACE AT THE RIGHT.*

1. I.   Listening skills are very important for managers.   1.____
    II.   Listening skills are not usually emphasized.
    III. Whenever managers are depicted in books, manuals or the media, they are always talking, never listening.
    IV. We'd like you to read the enclosed handout on listening skills and to try to consciously apply them this week.
    V.   We guarantee they will improve the quality of your interactions.

    A.   Unfortunately, listening skills are not usually emphasized for managers. Managers are always depicted as talking, never listening. We'd like you to read the enclosed handout on listening skills. Please try to apply these principles this week. If you do, we guarantee they will improve the quality of your interactions.
    B.   The enclosed handout on listening skills will be important improving the quality of your interactions. We guarantee it. All you have to do is take some time this week to read it and to consciously try to apply the principles. Listening skills are very important for managers, but they are not usually emphasized. Whenever managers are depicted in books, manuals or the media, they are always talking, never listening.
    C.   Listening well is one of the most important skills a manager can have, yet it's not usually given much attention. Think about any representation of managers in books, manuals, or in the media that you may have seen. They're always talking, never listening. We'd like you to read the enclosed handout on listening skills and consciously try to apply them the rest of the week. We guarantee you will see a difference in the quality of your interactions.
    D.   Effective listening, one very important tool in the effective manager's arsenal, is usually not emphasized enough. The usual depiction of managers in books, manuals or the media is one in which they are always talking, never listening. We'd like you to read the enclosed handout and consciously try to apply the information contained therein throughout the rest of the week. We feel sure that you will see a marked difference in the quality of your interactions.

2.   I.   Chekhov wrote three dramatic masterpieces which share certain themes and for-   2.____
mats: <u>Uncle Vanya</u>, <u>The Cherry Orchard</u>, and <u>The Three Sisters</u>.

    II.   They are primarily concerned with the passage of time and how this erodes
human aspirations.

    III.   The plays are haunted by the ghosts of the wasted life.

    IV.   The characters are concerned with life's lesser problems; however, such as the
inability to make decisions, loyalty to the wrong cause, and the inability to be
clear.

    V.   This results in a sweet, almost aching, type of a sadness referred to as Chek-
hovian.

    A.   Chekhov wrote three dramatic masterpieces: Uncle <u>Vanya</u>, <u>The Cherry Orchard,</u>
and <u>The Three Sisters</u>. These masterpieces share certain themes and formats: the
passage of time, how time erodes human aspirations, and the ghosts of wasted
life. Each masterpiece is characterized by a sweet, almost aching, type of sadness
that has become known as Chekhovian. The sweetness of this sadness hinges on
the fact that it is not the great tragedies of life which are destroying these characters, but their minor flaws: indecisiveness, misplaced loyalty, unclarity.

    B.   <u>The Cherry Orchard</u>, <u>Uncle Vanya</u>, and <u>The Three Sisters</u> are three dramatic mas-
terpieces written by Chekhov that use similar formats to explore a common theme.
Each is primarily concerned with the way that passing time wears down human
aspirations, and each is haunted by the ghosts of the wasted life. The characters
are shown struggling futilely with the lesser problems of life: indecisiveness, loyalty
to the wrong cause, and the inability to be clear. These struggles create a mood of
sweet, almost aching, sadness that has become known as Chekhovian.

    C.   Chekhov's dramatic masterpieces are, along with <u>The Cherry Orchard</u>, <u>Uncle
Vanya</u>, and The Three Sisters. These plays share certain thematic and formal simi-
larities. They are concerned most of all with the passage of time and the way in
which time erodes human aspirations. Each play is haunted by the specter of the
wasted life. Chekhov's characters are caught, however, by life's lesser snares:
indecisiveness, loyalty to the wrong cause, and unclarity. The characteristic mood
is a sweet, almost aching type of sadness that has come to be known as Chekhovian.

    D.   A Chekhovian mood is characterized by sweet, almost aching, sadness. The term
comes from three dramatic tragedies by Chekhov which revolve around the sadness of a wasted life. The three masterpieces (<u>Uncle Vanya</u>, <u>The Three Sisters</u>,
and <u>The Cherry Orchard)</u> share the same theme and format. The plays are concerned with how the passage of time erodes human aspirations. They are peopled
with characters who are struggling with life's lesser problems. These are people
who are indecisive, loyal to the wrong causes, or are unable to make themselves
clear.

3. I. Movie previews have often helped producers decide what parts of movies they should take out or leave in.
    II. The first 1933 preview of <u>King Kong</u> was very helpful to the producers because many people ran screaming from the theater and would not return when four men first attacked by Kong were eaten by giant spiders.
    III. The 1950 premiere of Sunset Boulevard resulted in the filming of an entirely new beginning, and a delay of six months in the film's release.
    IV. In the original opening scene, William Holden was in a morgue talking with thirty-six other "corpses" about the ways some of them had died.
    V. When he began to tell them of his life with Gloria Swanson, the audience found this hilarious, instead of taking the scene seriously.

    A. Movie previews have often helped producers decide what parts of movies they should leave in or take out. For example, the first preview of <u>King Kong</u> in 1933 was very helpful. In one scene, four men were first attacked by Kong and then eaten by giant spiders. Many members of the audience ran screaming from the theater and would not return. The premiere of the 1950 film <u>Sunset Boulevard</u> was also very helpful. In the original opening scene, William Holden was in a morgue with thirty-six other "corpses," discussing the ways some of them had died. When he began to tell them of his life with Gloria Swanson, the audience found this hilarious. They were supposed to take the scene seriously. The result was a delay of six months in the release of the film while a new beginning was added.
    B. Movie previews have often helped producers decide whether they should change various parts of a movie. After the 1933 preview of <u>King Kong,</u> a scene in which four men who had been attacked by Kong were eaten by giant spiders was taken out as many people ran screaming from the theater and would not return. The 1950 premiere of <u>Sunset Boulevard</u> also led to some changes. In the original opening scene, William Holden was in a morgue talking with thirty-six other "corpses" about the ways some of them had died. When he began to tell them of his life with Gloria Swanson, the audience found this hilarious, instead of taking the scene seriously.
    C. What do <u>Sunset Boulevard</u> and <u>King Kong</u> have in common? Both show the value of using movie previews to test audience reaction. The first 1933 preview of <u>King Kong</u> showed that a scene showing four men being eaten by giant spiders after having been attacked by Kong was too frightening for many people. They ran screaming from the theater and couldn't be coaxed back. The 1950 premiere of <u>Sunset Boulevard</u> was also a scream, but not the kind the producers intended. The movie opens with William Holden lying in a morgue discussing the ways they had died with thirty-six other "corpses." When he began to tell them of his life with Gloria Swanson, the audience couldn't take him seriously. Their laughter caused a six-month delay while the beginning was rewritten.
    D. Producers very often use movie previews to decide if changes are needed. The premiere of <u>Sunset Boulevard</u> in 1950 led to a new beginning and a six-month delay in film release. At the beginning, William Holden and thirty-six other "corpses" discuss the ways some of them died. Rather than taking this seriously, the audience thought it was hilarious when he began to tell them of his life with Gloria Swanson. The first 1933 preview of <u>King Kong</u> was very helpful for its producers because one scene so terrified the audience that many of them ran screaming from the theater and would not return. In this particular scene, four men who had first been attacked by Kong were being eaten by giant spiders.

4. I. It is common for supervisors to view employees as "things" to be manipulated.   4.____
    II. This approach does not motivate employees, nor does the carrot-and-stick approach because employees often recognize these behaviors and resent them.
    III. Supervisors can change these behaviors by using self-inquiry and persistence.
    IV. The best managers genuinely respect those they work with, are supportive and helpful, and are interested in working as a team with those they supervise.
    V. They disagree with the Golden Rule that says "he or she who has the gold makes the rules."

A. Some managers act as if they think the Golden Rule means "he or she who has the gold makes the rules." They show disrespect to employees by seeing them as "things" to be manipulated. Obviously, this approach does not motivate employees any more than the carrot-and-stick approach motivates them. The employees are smart enough to spot these behaviors and resent them. On the other hand, the managers genuinely respect those they work with, are supportive and helpful, and are interested in working as a team. Self-inquiry and persistence can change even the former type of supervisor into the latter.

B. Many supervisors fall into the trap of viewing employees as "things" to be manipulated, or try to motivate them by using a earrot-and-stick approach. These methods do not motivate employees, who often recognize the behaviors and resent them. Supervisors can change these behaviors, however, by using self-inquiry and persistence. The best managers are supportive and helpful, and have genuine respect for those with whom they work. They are interested in working as a team with those they supervise. To them, the Golden Rule is not "he or she who has the gold makes the rules."

C. Some supervisors see employees as "things" to be used or manipulated using a carrot-and-stick technique. These methods don't work. Employees often see through them and resent them. A supervisor who wants to change may do so. The techniques of self-inquiry and persistence can be used to turn him or her into the type of supervisor who doesn't think the Golden Rule is "he or she who has the gold makes the rules." They may become like the best managers who treat those with whom they work with respect and give them help and support. These are the managers who know how to build a team.

D. Unfortunately, many supervisors act as if their employees are objects whose movements they can position at will. This mistaken belief has the same result as another popular motivational technique—the carrot-and-stick approach. Both attitudes can lead to the same result — resentment from those employees who recognize the behaviors for what they are. Supervisors who recognize these behaviors can change through the use of persistence and the use of self-inquiry. It's important to remember that the best managers respect their employees. They readily give necessary help and support and are interested in working as a team with those they supervise. To these managers, the Golden Rule is not "he or she who has the gold makes the rules."

5.   I.   The first half of the nineteenth century produced a group of pessimistic poets —
        Byron, De Musset, Heine, Pushkin, and Leopardi.

   II.   It also produced a group of pessimistic composers—Schubert, Chopin, Schu-
        mann, and even the later Beethoven.

   III. Above all, in philosophy, there was the profoundly pessimistic philosopher,
        Schopenhauer.

   IV. The Revolution was dead, the Bourbons were restored, the feudal barons were
        reclaiming their land, and progress everywhere was being suppressed, as the
        great age was over.

   V.   "I thank God," said Goethe, "that I am not young in so thoroughly finished a
        world."

   A.   "I thank God," said Goethe, "that I am not young in so thoroughly finished a world."
The Revolution was dead, the Bourbons were restored, the feudal barons were
reclaiming their land, and progress everywhere was being suppressed. The first
half of the nineteenth century produced a group of pessimistic poets: Byron, De
Musset, Heine, Pushkin, and Leopardi. It also produced pessimistic composers:
Schubert, Chopin, Schumann. Although Beethoven came later, he fits into this
group, too. Finally and above all, it also produced a profoundly pessimistic philosopher, Schopenhauer. The great age was over.

   B.   The first half of the nineteenth century produced a group of pessimistic poets:
Byron, De Musset, Heine, Pushkin, and Leopardi. It produced a group of pessimistic composers: Schubert, Chopin, Schumann, and even the later Beethoven.
Above all, it produced a profoundly pessimistic philosopher, Schopenhauer. For
each of these men, the great age was over. The Revolution was dead, and the
Bourbons were restored. The feudal barons were reclaiming their land, and
progress everywhere was being suppressed.

   C.   The great age was over. The Revolution was dead—the Bourbons were restored,
and the feudal barons were reclaiming their land. Progress everywhere was being
suppressed. Out of this climate came a profound pessimism. Poets, like Byron, De
Musset, Heine, Pushkin, and Leopardi; composers, like Schubert, Chopin, Schumann, and even the later Beethoven; and, above all, a profoundly pessimistic philosopher, Schopenauer. This pessimism which arose in the first half of the
nineteenth century is illustrated by these words of Goethe, "I thank God that I am
not young in so thoroughly finished a world."

   D.   The first half of the nineteenth century produced a group of pessimistic poets,
Byron, De Musset, Heine, Pushkin, and Leopardi — and a group of pessimistic
composers, Schubert, Chopin, Schumann, and the later Beethoven. Above all, it
produced a profoundly pessimistic philosopher, Schopenhauer. The great age was
over. The Revolution was dead, the Bourbons were restored, the feudal barons
were reclaiming their land, and progress everywhere was being suppressed. "I
thank God," said Goethe, "that I am not young in so thoroughly finished a world."

6.   I.   A new manager sometimes may feel insecure about his or her competence in the
        new position.

   II.   The new manager may then exhibit defensive or arrogant behavior towards
        those one supervises, or the new manager may direct overly flattering behavior
        toward one's new supervisor.

A. Sometimes, a new manager may feel insecure about his or her ability to perform well in this new position. The insecurity may lead him or her to treat others differently. He or she may display arrogant or defensive behavior towards those he or she supervises, or be overly flattering to his or her new supervisor.

B. A new manager may sometimes feel insecure about his or her ability to perform well in the new position. He or she may then become arrogant, defensive, or overly flattering towards those he or she works with.

C. There are times when a new manager may be insecure about how well he or she can perform in the new job. The new manager may also behave defensive or act in an arrogant way towards those he or she supervises, or overly flatter his or her boss.

D. Sometimes, a new manager may feel insecure about his or her ability to perform well in the new position. He or she may then display arrogant or defensive behavior towards those they supervise, or become overly flattering towards their supervisors.

7. I. It is possible to eliminate unwanted behavior by bringing it under stimulus control — tying the behavior to a cue, and then never, or rarely, giving the cue.

II. One trainer successfully used this method to keep an energetic young porpoise from coming out of her tank whenever she felt like it, which was potentially dangerous.

III. Her trainer taught her to do it for a reward, in response to a hand signal, and then rarely gave the signal.

7.____

A. Unwanted behavior can be eliminated by tying the behavior to a cue, and then never, or rarely, giving the cue. This is called stimulus control. One trainer was able to use this method to keep an energetic young porpoise from coming out of her tank by teaching her to come out for a reward in response to a hand signal, and then rarely giving the signal.

B. Stimulus control can be used to eliminate unwanted behavior. In this method, behavior is tied to a cue, and then the cue is rarely, if ever, given. One trainer was able to successfully use stimulus control to keep an energetic young porpoise from coming out of her tank whenever she felt like it — a potentially dangerous practice. She taught the porpoise to come out for a reward when she gave a hand signal, and then rarely gave the signal.

C. It is possible to eliminate behavior that is undesirable by bringing it under stimulus control by tying behavior to a signal, and then rarely giving the signal. One trainer successfully used this method to keep an energetic young porpoise from coming out of her tank, a potentially dangerous situation. Her trainer taught the porpoise to do it for a reward, in response to a hand signal, and then would rarely give the signal.

D. By using stimulus control, it is possible to eliminate unwanted behavior by tying the behavior to a cue, and then rarely or never give the cue. One trainer was able to use this method to successfully stop a young porpoise from coming out of her tank whenever she felt like it. To curb this potentially dangerous practice, the porpoise was taught by the trainer to come out of the tank for a reward, in response to a hand signal, and then rarely given the signal.

8.   I.   There is a great deal of concern over the safety of commercial trucks, caused by   8.____
          their greatly increased role in serious accidents since federal deregulation in 1981.
     II. Recently, 60 percent of trucks in New York and Connecticut and 70 percent of
          trucks in Maryland randomly stopped by state troopers failed safety inspections.
     III. Sixteen states in the United States require no training at all for truck drivers.

     A.   Since federal deregulation in 1981, there has been a great deal of concern over the
          safety of commercial trucks, and their greatly increased role in serious accidents.
          Recently, 60 percent of trucks in New York and Connecticut, and 70 percent of
          trucks in Maryland failed safety inspections. Sixteen states in the United States
          require no training at all for truck drivers.
     B.   There is a great deal of concern over the safety of commercial trucks since federal
          deregulation in 1981. Their role in serious accidents has greatly increased.
          Recently, 60 percent of trucks randomly stopped in Connecticut and New York, and
          70 percent in Maryland failed safety inspections conducted by state troopers. Six-
          teen states in the United States provide no training at all for truck drivers.
     C.   Commercial trucks have a greatly increased role in serious accidents since federal
          deregulation in 1981. This has led to a great deal of concern. Recently, 70 percent
          of trucks in Maryland and 60 percent of trucks in New York and Connecticut failed
          inspection of those that were randomly stopped by state troopers. Sixteen states in
          the United States require no training for all truck drivers.
     D.   Since federal deregulation in 1981, the role that commercial trucks have played in
          serious accidents has greatly increased, and this has led to a great deal of con-
          cern. Recently, 60 percent of trucks in New York and Connecticut, and 70 percent
          of trucks in Maryland randomly stopped by state troopers failed safety inspections.
          Sixteen states in the U.S. don't require any training for truck drivers.

9.   I.   No matter how much some people have, they still feel unsatisfied and want more,   9.____
          or want to keep what they have forever.
     II. One recent television documentary showed several people flying from New York
          to Paris for a one-day shopping spree to buy platinum earrings, because they
          were bored.
     III. In Brazil, some people are ordering coffins that cost a minimum of $45,000 and
          are equipping them with deluxe stereos, televisions and other graveyard neces-
          sities.

     A.   Some people, despite having a great deal, still feel unsatisfied and want more, or
          think they can keep what they have forever. One recent documentary on television
          showed several people enroute from Paris to New York for a one day shopping
          spree to buy platinum earrings, because they were bored. Some people in Brazil
          are even ordering coffins equipped with such graveyard necessities as deluxe ste-
          reos and televisions. The price of the coffins start at $45,000.
     B.   No matter how much some people have, they may feel unsatisfied. This leads them
          to want more, or to want to keep what they have forever. Recently, a television doc-
          umentary depicting several people flying from New York to Paris for a one day
          shopping spree to buy platinum earrings. They were bored. Some people in Brazil
          are ordering coffins that cost at least $45,000 and come equipped with deluxe tele-
          visions, stereos and other necessary graveyard items.
     C.   Some people will be dissatisfied no matter how much they have. They may want
          more, or they may want to keep what they have forever. One recent television doc-
          umentary showed several people, motivated by boredom, jetting from New York to

Paris for a one-day shopping spree to buy platinum earrings. In Brazil, some people are ordering coffins equipped with deluxe stereos, televisions and other graveyard necessities. The minimum price for these coffins - $45,000.

D. Some people are never satisfied. No matter how much they have they still want more, or think they can keep what they have forever. One television documentary recently showed several people flying from New York to Paris for the day to buy platinum earrings because they were bored. In Brazil, some people are ordering coffins that cost $45,000 and are equipped with deluxe stereos, televisions and other graveyard necessities.

10.   I. A television signal or Video signal has three parts.   10._____
        II. Its parts are the black-and-white portion, the color portion, and the synchronizing (sync) pulses, which keep the picture stable.
        III. Each video source, whether it's a camera or a video-cassette recorder, contains its own generator of these synchronizing pulses to accompany the picture that it's sending in order to keep it steady and straight.
        IV. In order to produce a clean recording, a video-cassette recorder must "lock-up" to the sync pulses that are part of the video it is trying to record, and this effort may be very noticeable if the device does not have genlock.

        A. There are three parts to a television or video signal: the black-and-white part, the color part, and the synchronizing (sync) pulses, which keep the picture stable. Whether it's a video-cassette recorder or a camera, each each video source contains its own pulse that synchronizes and generates the picture it's sending in order to keep it straight and steady. A video-cassette recorder must "lock up" to the sync pulses that are part of the video it's trying to record. If the device doesn't have genlock, this effort must be very noticeable.

        B. A video signal or television is comprised of three parts: the black-and-white portion, the color portion, and the the sync (synchronizing) pulses, which keep the picture stable. Whether it's a camera or a video-cassette recorder, each video source contains its own generator of these synchronizing pulses. These accompany the picture that it's sending in order to keep it straight and steady. A video-cassette recorder must "lock up" to the sync pulses that are part of the video it is trying to record in order to produce a clean recording. This effort may be very noticeable if the device does not have genlock.

        C. There are three parts to a television or video signal: the color portion, the black-and-white portion, and the sync (synchronizing pulses). These keep the picture stable. Each video source, whether it's a video-cassette recorder or a camera, generates these synchronizing pulses accompanying the picture it's sending in order to keep it straight and steady. If a clean recording is to be produced, a video-cassette recorder must store the sync pulses that are part of the video it is trying to record. This effort may not be noticeable if the device does not have genlock.

        D. A television signal or video signal has three parts: the black-and-white portion, the color portion, and the synchronizing (sync) pulses. It's the sync pulses which keep the picture stable, which accompany it and keep it steady and straight. Whether it's a camera or a video-cassette recorder, each video source contains its own generator of these synchronizing pulses. To produce a clean recording, a video-cassette recorder must "lock-up" to the sync pulses that are part of the video it is trying to record. If the device does not have genlock, this effort may be very noticeable.

KEY (CORRECT ANSWERS)

1.	C	6.	A
2.	B	7.	B
3.	A	8.	D
4.	B	9.	C
5.	D	10.	D

———

PREPARING WRITTEN MATERIAL

EXAMINATION SECTION
TEST 1

DIRECTIONS: Each of the sentences in the Tests that follow may be classified under one of the following four categories:

    A. *Faulty* because of incorrect grammar or word usage
    B. *Faulty* because of incorrect punctuation
    C. *Faulty* because of incorrect capitalization or incorrect spelling
    D. *Correct*

Examine each sentence carefully to determine under which of the above four options it is best classified. Then, in the space to the right, print the capital letter preceding the option which is the best of the four suggested above.

(Note that each faulty sentence contains but one type of error. Consider a sentence to be correct if it contains none of the types of errors mentioned, even though there may be other correct ways of expressing the same thought.)

1. He sent the notice to the clerk who you hired yesterday.   1._____

2. It must be admitted, however that you were not informed of this change.   2._____

3. Only the employees who have served in this grade for at least two years are eligible for promotion.   3._____

4. The work was divided equally between she and Mary.   4._____

5. He thought that you were not available at that time.   5._____

6. When the messenger returns; please give him this package.   6._____

7. The new secretary prepared, typed, addressed, and delivered, the notices.   7._____

8. Walking into the room, his desk can be seen at the rear.   8._____

9. Although John has worked here longer than She, he produces a smaller amount of work.   9._____

10. She said she could of typed this report yesterday.   10.

11. Neither one of these procedures are adequate for the efficient performance of this task.   11._____

12. The typewriter is the tool of the typist; the cashe register, the tool of the cashier.   12._____

13. "The assignment must be completed as soon as possible" said the supervisor.   13._____

14. As you know, office handbooks are issued to all new Employees.   14._____

15. Writing a speech is sometimes easier than to deliver it before an audience.   15._____

16. Mr. Brown our accountant, will audit the accounts next week.   16._____

17. Give the assignment to whomever is able to do it most efficiently.

17._____

18. The supervisor expected either your or I to file these reports.

18._____

KEY (CORRECT ANSWERS)

1.	A	10.	A
2.	B	11.	A
3.	D	12.	C
4.	A	13.	B
5.	D	14.	C
6.	B	15.	A
7.	B	16.	B
8.	A	17.	A
9.	C	18.	A

TEST 2

DIRECTIONS: Each of the sentences in the Tests that follow may be classified under one of
the following four categories:
A. *Faulty* because of incorrect grammar or word usage
B. *Faulty* because of incorrect punctuation
C. *Faulty* because of incorrect capitalization or incorrect spelling
D. *Correct*

Examine each sentence carefully to determine under which of the above four options it is
best classified. Then, in the space to the right, print the capital letter preceding the option
which is the best of the four suggested above.

Note that each faulty sentence contains but one type of error. Consider a sentence to be
correct if it contains none of the types of errors mentioned, even though there may be other
correct ways of expressing the same thought.)

1.   The fire apparently started in the storeroom, which is usually locked.   1._____

2.   On approaching the victim two bruises were noticed by this officer.   2._____

3.   The officer, who was there examined the report with great care.   3._____

4.   Each employee in the office had a seperate desk.   4._____

5.   All employees including members of the clerical staff, were invited to the lecture. 5._____

6.   The suggested Procedure is similar to the one now in use.   6._____

7.   No one was more pleased with the new procedure than the chauffeur.   7._____

8.   He tried to persaude her to change the procedure.   8._____

9.   The total of the expenses charged to petty cash were high.   9._____

10. An understanding between him and I was finally reached.   10._____

KEY (CORRECT ANSWERS)

1. D 6. C
2. A 7. D
3. B 8. C
4. C 9. A
5. B 10. A

————

TEST 3

DIRECTIONS: Each of the sentences in the Tests that follow may be classified under one of the following four categories:
- A. *Faulty* because of incorrect grammar or word usage
- B. *Faulty* because of incorrect punctuation
- C. *Faulty* because of incorrect capitalization or incorrect spelling
- D. *Correct*

Examine each sentence carefully to determine under which of the above four options it is best classified. Then, in the space to the right, print the capital letter preceding the option which is the best of the four suggested above.

(Note that each faulty sentence contains but one type of error. Consider a sentence to be correct if it contains none of the types of errors mentioned, even though there may be other correct ways of expressing the same thought.)

1. They told both he and *I* that the prisoner had escaped.   1.____

2. Any superior officer, who, disregards the just complaints of his subordinates, is remiss in the performance of his duty.   2.____

3. Only those members of the national organization who resided in the Middle West attended the conference in Chicago.   3.____

4. We told him to give the investigation assignment to whoever was available.   4.____

5. Please do not disappoint and embarass us by not appearing in court.   5.____

6. Although the officer's speech proved to be entertaining, the topic was not relevent to the main theme of the conference.   6.____

7. In February all new officers attended a training course in which they were learned in their principal duties and the fundamental operating procedures of the department.   7.____

8. I personally seen inmate Jones threaten inmates Smith and Green with bodily harm if they refused to participate in the plot.   8.____

9. To the layman, who on a chance visit to the prison observes everything functioning smoothly, the maintenance of prison discipline may seem to be a relatively easily realizable objective.   9.____

10. The prisoners in cell block fourty were forbidden to sit on the cell cots during the recreation hour.   10.____

KEY (CORRECT ANSWERS)

1.	A	6.	C
2.	B	7.	A
3.	C	8.	A
4.	D	9.	D
5.	C	10.	C

———

TEST 4

DIRECTIONS: Each of the sentences in the Tests that follow may be classified under one of the following four categories:
- A. *Faulty* because of incorrect grammar or word usage
- B. *Faulty* because of incorrect punctuation
- C. *Faulty* because of incorrect capitalization or incorrect spelling
- D. *Correct*

Examine each sentence carefully to determine under which of the above four options it is best classified. Then, in the space to the right, print the capital letter preceding the option which is the best of the four suggested above.

(Note that each faulty sentence contains but one type of error. Consider a sentence to be correct if it contains none of the types of errors mentioned, even though there may be other correct ways of expressing the same thought.)

1. I cannot encourage you any.   1._____

2. You always look well in those sort of clothes.   2._____

3. Shall we go to the park?   3._____

4. The man whome he introduced was Mr. Carey.   4._____

5. She saw the letter laying here this morning.   5._____

6. It should rain before the Afternoon is over.   6._____

7. They have already went home.   7._____

8. That Jackson will be elected is evident.   8._____

9. He does not hardly approve of us.   9._____

10. It was he, who won the prize.   10._____

KEY (CORRECT ANSWERS)

1.	A		6.	C
2.	A		7.	A
3.	D		8.	D
4.	C		9.	A
5.	A		10.	B

———

TEST 5

DIRECTIONS: Each of the sentences in the Tests that follow may be classified under one of the following four categories:

DIRECTIONS: Each of the sentences in the Tests that follow may be classified under one of the following four categories:
      A. *Faulty* because of incorrect grammar or word usage
      B. *Faulty* because of incorrect punctuation
      C. *Faulty* because of incorrect capitalization or incorrect spelling
      D. *Correct*

Examine each sentence carefully to determine under which of the above four options it is best classified. Then, in the space to the right, print the capital letter preceding the option which is the best of the four suggested above.

Note that each faulty sentence contains but one type of error. Consider a sentence to be correct if it contains none of the types of errors mentioned, even though there may be other correct ways of expressing the same thought.)

1. Shall we go to the park.   1._____

2. They are, alike, in this particular.   2._____

3. They gave the poor man sume food when he knocked on the door.   3._____

4. I regret the loss caused by the error.   4._____

5. The students' will have a new teacher.   5._____

6. They sweared to bring out all the facts.   6._____

7. He decided to open a branch store on 33rd street.   7._____

8. His speed is equal and more than that of a racehorse.   8._____

9. He felt very warm on that Summer day.   9._____

10. He was assisted by his friend, who lives in the next house.   10._____

———

KEY (CORRECT ANSWERS)

1.	B	6.	A
2.	B	7.	C
3.	C	8.	A
4.	D	9.	C
5.	B	10.	D

————

TEST 6

DIRECTIONS: Each of the sentences in the Tests that follow may be classified under one of the following four categories:

DIRECTIONS: Each of the sentences in the Tests that follow may be classified under one of the following four categories:
     A. *Faulty* because of incorrect grammar or word usage
     B. *Faulty* because of incorrect punctuation
     C. *Faulty* because of incorrect capitalization or incorrect spelling
     D. *Correct*

Examine each sentence carefully to determine under which of the above four options it is best classified. Then, in the space to the right, print the capital letter preceding the option which is the best of the four suggested above.

Note that each faulty sentence contains but one type of error. Consider a sentence to be correct if it contains none of the types of errors mentioned, even though there may be other correct ways of expressing the same thought.)

1. The climate of New York is colder than California.   1.____

2. I shall wait for you on the corner.   2.____

3. Did we see the boy who, we think, is the leader.   3.____

4. Being a modest person, John seldom talks about his invention .   4.____

5. The gang is called the smith street boys.   5.____

6. He seen the man break into the store.   6.____

7. We expected to lay still there for quite a while.   7.____

8. He is considered to be the Leader of his organization.   8.____

9. Although I recieved an invitation, I won't go.   9.____

10. The letter must be here some place.   10.____

KEY (CORRECT ANSWERS)

1.	A	6.	A
2.	D	7.	A
3.	B	8.	C
4.	D	9.	C
5.	C	10.	A

———

TEST 7

DIRECTIONS: Each of the sentences in the Tests that follow may be classified under one of the following four categories:

DIRECTIONS: Each of the sentences in the Tests that follow may be classified under one of the following four categories:
      A.   *Faulty* because of incorrect grammar or word usage
      B.   *Faulty* because of incorrect punctuation
      C.   *Faulty* because of incorrect capitalization or incorrect spelling
      D.   *Correct*

Examine each sentence carefully to determine under which of the above four options it is best classified. Then, in the space to the right, print the capital letter preceding the option which is the best of the four suggested above.

Note that each faulty sentence contains but one type of error. Consider a sentence to be correct if it contains none of the types of errors mentioned, even though there may be other correct ways of expressing the same thought.)

1.   I though it to be he.   1._____

2.   We expect to remain here for a long time.   2._____

3.   The committee was agreed.   3._____

4.   Two-thirds of the building are finished.   4._____

5.   The water was froze.   5._____

6.   Everyone of the salesmen must supply their own car.   6._____

7.   Who is the author of Gone With the Wind?   7._____

8.   He marched on and declaring that he would never surrender.   8._____

9.   Who shall I say called?   9._____

10.   Everyone has left but they.   10._____

KEY (CORRECT ANSWERS)

1.	A		6.	A
2.	D		7.	B
3.	D		8.	A
4.	A		9.	D
5.	A		10.	D

———

TEST 8

DIRECTIONS: Each of the sentences in the Tests that follow may be classified under one of the following four categories:

DIRECTIONS: Each of the sentences in the Tests that follow may be classified under one of the following four categories:
        A. *Faulty* because of incorrect grammar or word usage
        B. *Faulty* because of incorrect punctuation
        C. *Faulty* because of incorrect capitalization or incorrect spelling
        D. *Correct*

Examine each sentence carefully to determine under which of the above four options it is best classified. Then, in the space to the right, print the capital letter preceding the option which is the best of the four suggested above.

Note that each faulty sentence contains but one type of error. Consider a sentence to be correct if it contains none of the types of errors mentioned, even though there may be other correct ways of expressing the same thought.)

1. Who did we give the order to?   1.____

2. Send your order in immediately.   2.____

3. I believe I paid the Bill.   3.____

4. I have not met but one person.   4.____

5. Why aren't Tom, and Fred, going to the dance?   5.____

6. What reason is there for him not going?   6.____

7. The seige of Malta was a tremendous event.   7.____

8. I was there yesterday I assure you.   8.____

9. Your ukelele is better than mine.   9.____

10. No one was there only Mary.   10.____

KEY (CORRECT ANSWERS)

1.	A		6.	A
2.	D		7.	C
3.	C		8.	B
4.	A		9.	C
5.	B		10.	A

———

TEST 9

DIRECTIONS: In each of the following groups of sentences, one of the four sentences is faulty in grammar, punctuation, or capitalization. Select the incorrect sentence in each case.

1. A. If you had stood at home and done your homework, you would not have failed in arithmetic.
    B. Her affected manner annoyed every member of the audience.
    C. How will the new law affect our income taxes?
    D. The plants were not affected by the long, cold winter, but they succumbed to the drought of summer.

    1.____

2. A. He is one of the most able men who have been in the Senate.
    B. It is he who is to blame for the lamentable mistake.
    C. Haven't you a helpful suggestion to make at this time?
    D. The money was robbed from the blind man's cup.

    2.____

3. A. The amount of children in this school is steadily increasing.
    B. After taking an apple from the table, she went out to play.
    C. He borrowed a dollar from me.
    D. I had hoped my brother would arrive before me.

    3.____

4. A. Whom do you think I hear from every week?
    B. Who do you think is the right man for the job?
    C. Who do you think I found in the room?
    D. He is the man whom we considered a good candidate for the presidency.

    4.____

5. A. Quietly the puppy laid down before the fireplace.
    B. You have made your bed; now lie in it.
    C. I was badly sunburned because I had lain too long in the sun.
    D. I laid the doll on the bed and left the room.

    5.____

———

KEY (CORRECT ANSWERS)

1. A
2. D
3. A
4. C
5. A

———

INTERPRETING STATISTICAL DATA
GRAPHS, CHARTS AND TABLES
TEST 1

DIRECTIONS: Each question or incomplete statement is followed by several suggested answers or completions. Select the one that BEST answers the question or completes the statement. *PRINT THE LETTER OF THE CORRECT ANSWER IN THE SPACE AT THE RIGHT.*

Questions 1-5.

DIRECTIONS: Questions 1 through 5 are to be answered SOLELY on the basis of the following chart.

| | DATES | | | | | NO. OF COPIES OF | |
JOB. NO.	Submitted	Required	Completed	PROCESS	NO. OF ORIGINALS	EACH ORIGINAL	REQUEST- ING UNIT
324	6/22	6/25	6/25	Xerox	14	25	Research
325	6/25	6/27	6/28	Kodak	10	125	Training
326	6/25	6/25	6/25	Xerox	12	11	Budget
327	6/25	6/27	6/26	Press	17	775	Admin. Div. H
328	6/28	ASAP*	6/25	Press	5	535	Personnel
329	6/26	6/26	6/27	Xerox	15	8	Admin. Div. G

DUPLICATION JOBS

*ASAP - As soon as possible

1.   The unit whose job was to be xeroxed but was NOT completed by the date required is   1.____

    A.   Administrative Division H
    B.   Administrative Division G
    C.   Research
    D.   Training

2.   The job with the LARGEST number of original pages to be xeroxed is job number   2.____

    A. 324   B. 326   C. 327   D. 329

3. Jobs were completed AFTER June 26, for

    A. Training and Administrative Division G
    B. Training and Administrative Division H
    C. Research and Budget
    D. Administrative Division G *only*

4. Which one of the following units submitted a job which was completed SOONER than required?

    A. Training
    B. Administrative Division H
    C. Personnel
    D. Administrative Division G

5. The jobs which were submitted on different days but were completed on the SAME day and used the SAME process had job numbers

    A. 324 and 326
    C. 324, 326, and 328
    B. 327 and 328
    D. 324, 326, and 329

KEY (CORRECT ANSWERS)

1. B
2. D
3. A
4. B
5. A

TEST 2

Questions 1-10.

DIRECTIONS: Questions 1 through 10 are to be answered SOLELY on the basis of the Production Record table shown below for the Information Unit in Agency X for the work week ended Friday, December 6. The table shows, for each employee, the quantity of each type of work performed and the percentage of the work week spent in performing each type of work.

NOTE: Assume that each employee works 7 hours a day and 5 days a week, making a total of 35 hours for the work week.

PRODUCTION RECORD - INFORMATION UNIT IN AGENCY X
(For the work week ended Friday, December 6)

| | NUMBER OF | | | |
	Papers Filed	Sheets Proofread	Visitors Received	Envelopes Addressed
Miss Agar	3120	33	178	752
Mr. Brun	1565	59	252	724
Miss Case	2142	62	214	426
Mr. Dale	4259	29	144	1132
Miss Earl	2054	58	212	878
Mr. Farr	1610	69	245	621
Miss Glen	2390	57	230	790
Mr. Hope	3425	32	176	805
Miss Iver	3726	56	148	650
Mr. Joad	3212	55	181	495

| | PERCENTAGE OF WORK WEEK SPENT ON | | | | |
	Filing Papers	Proof-reading	Receiving Visitors	Addressing Envelopes	Performing Miscellaneous Work
Miss Agar	30%	9%	34%	11%	16%
Mr. Brun	13%	15%	52%	10%	10%
Miss Case	23%	18%	38%	6%	15%
Mr. Dale	50%	7%	17%	16%	10%
Miss Earl	24%	14%	37%	14%	11%
Mr. Farr	16%	19%	48%	8%	9%
Miss Glenn	27%	12%	42%	12%	7%
Mr. Hope	38%	8%	32%	13%	9%
Miss Iver	43%	13%	24%	9%	11%
Mr. Joad	33%	11%	36%	7%	13%

1. For the week, the average amount of time which the employees spent in proofreading was MOST NEARLY _____ hours.   1.__

   A. 3.1   B. 3.6   C. 4.4   D. 5.1

2. The average number of visitors received daily by an employee was MOST NEARLY   2.__

   A. 40   B. 57   C. 198   D. 395

3. Of the following employees, the one who addressed envelopes at the FASTEST rate was   3.__

   A. Miss Agar   B. Mr. Brun   C. Miss Case   D. Mr. Dale

4. Mr. Farr's rate of filing papers was MOST NEARLY _____ pages per minute.   4.__

   A. 2   B. 1.7   C. 5   D. 12

5. The average number of hours that Mr. Brun spent daily on receiving visitors exceeded the average number of hours that Miss Iver spent daily on the same type of work by MOST NEARLY _____ hours.   5.__

   A. 2   B. 3   C. 4   D. 5

6. Miss Earl worked at a FASTER rate than Miss Glen in   6.__

   A. filing papers   B. proofreading sheets
   C. receiving visitors   D. addressing envelopes

7. Mr. Joad's rate of filing papers _____ Miss Iver's rate of filing papers by APPROXI-MATELY _____ .   7.__

   A. was less than; 10%   B. exceeded; 33%
   C. was less than; 16%   D. exceeded; 12%

8. Assume that in the following week Miss Case is instructed to increase the percentage of her time spent on filing papers to 35%.
   If she continued to file papers at the same rate as she did for the week ended December 6, the number of additional papers that she filed the following week was MOST NEARLY   8.__

   A. 3260   B. 5400   C. 250   D. 1120

9. Assume that in the following week Mr. Hope increased his weekly total of envelopes addressed to 1092.
   If he continued to spend the same amount of time on this assignment as he did for the week ended December 6, the increase in his rate of addressing envelopes the following week was MOST NEARLY _____ envelopes per hour.   9.__

   A. 15   B. 65   C. 155   D. 240

10. Assume that in the following week Miss Agar and Mr. Dale spent 3 and 9 hours less, respectively, on filing papers than they had spent for the week ended December 6, without changing their rates of work.
The total number of papers filed during the following week by both Miss Agar and Mr. Dale was MOST NEARLY

   A. 4235   B. 4295   C. 4315   D. 4370

———

KEY (CORRECT ANSWERS)

1. C
2. A
3. B
4. C
5. A
6. C
7. D
8. D
9. B
10. B

———

TEST 3

Questions 1-6.

DIRECTIONS: Questions 1 through 6 are to be answered SOLELY on the basis of the chart below.

EMPLOYMENT ERRORS

	Allan	Barry	Cary	David
July	5	4	1	7
Aug.	8	3	9	8
Sept.	7	8	7	5
Oct.	3	6	5	3
Nov.	2	4	4	6
Dec.	5	2	8	4

1. The clerk with the HIGHEST number of errors for the 6-month period was   1.__

   A. Allan   B. Barry   C. Cary   D. David

2. If the number of errors made by Allan in the six months shown represented one-eighth of   2.__
   the total errors made by the unit during the entire year, what was the TOTAL number of
   errors made by the unit for the year?

   A. 124   B. 180   C. 240   D. 360

3. The number of errors made by David in November was what fraction of the total errors   3.__
   made in November?

   A. 1/3   B. 1/6   C. 378   D. 3/16

4. The average number of errors made per month per clerk was MOST NEARLY   4.__

   A. 4   B. 5   C. 6   D. 7

5. Of the total number of errors made during the six-month period, the percentage made in   5.__
   August was MOST NEARLY

   A. 2%   B. 4%   C. 23%   D. 44%

6. If the number of errors in the unit were to decrease in the next six months by 30%, what   6.__
   would be MOST NEARLY the total number of errors for the unit for the next six months?

   A. 87   B. 94   C. 120   D. 137

KEY (CORRECT ANSWERS)

1. C
2. C
3. C
4. B
5. C
6. A

TEST 4

Questions 1-5.

DIRECTIONS: Questions 1 through 5 are to be answered SOLELY on the basis of the data given below. These data show the performance rates of the employees in a particular division for a period of six months.

Employee	Jan.	Feb.	Mar.	April	May	June
A	96	53	64	48	76	72
B	84	58	69	56	67	79
C	73	68	71	54	59	62
D	98	74	79	66	86	74
E	89	78	67	74	75	77

1. According to the above data, the average monthly performance for a worker is MOST NEARLY

   A. 66   B. 69   C. 72   D. 75

1._____

2. According to the above data, the mean monthly performance for the division is MOST NEARLY

   A. 350   B. 358   C. 387   D. 429

2._____

3. According to the above data, the employee who shows the LEAST month-to-month variation in performance is

   A. A   B. B   C. C   D. D

3._____

4. According to the above data, the employee who shows the GREATEST range in performance is

   A. A   B. B   C. C   D. D

4._____

5. According to the above data, the median employee with respect to performance for the six-month period is

   A. A   B. B   C. C   D. D

5._____

KEY (CORRECT ANSWERS)

1. C
2. B
3. C
4. A
5. B

TEST 5

Questions 1-5.

DIRECTIONS: Questions 1 through 5 are to be answered SOLELY on the basis of the chart below, which shows the absences in Unit A for the period November 1 through November 15.

ABSENCE RECORD - UNIT A
November 1-15

Date:	1	2	3	4	5	6	7	8	9	10	11	12	13	14	15
Employee:															
Ames	X	s	H					X			H			X	X
Bloom	X		H			X	X	S	s	H	S	S			X
Deegan	X	J	H	J	J	J	X	X		H					X
Howard	X		H					X			H			X	X
Jergens	X	M	H	M	M	M		X			H			X	X
Lange	X		H			S	X	X							X
Morton	X						X	X	V	V	H				X
O'Shea	X		H			0		X			H	X		X	X

CODE FOR TYPES OF ABSENCE
X -   Saturday or Sunday
H -   Legal Holiday
P -   Leave without pay
M -   Military Leave
J -   Jury duty
V -   Vacation
S -   Sick Leave
O -   Other leave of absence

NOTE: If there is no entry against an employee's name under a date, the employee worked on that date.

1. According to the above chart, NO employee in Unit A was absent on

   A.   leave without pay
   C.   other leave of absence
   B.   military leave
   D.   vacation

2. According to the above chart, all but one of the employees in Unit A were present on the

   A.   3rd   B.   5th   C.   9th   D.   13th

3. According to the above chart, the ONLY employee who worked on a legal holiday when the other employees were absent are

   A.   Deegan and Morton
   C.   Lange and Morton
   B.   Howard and O'Shea
   D.   Morton and O'Shea

1.___

2.___

3.___

4. According to the above chart, the employee who was absent ONLY on a day that was a Saturday, Sunday, or legal holiday was

    4.____

    A. Bloom
    B. Howard
    C. G. Morton
    D. O'Shea

5. The employees who had more absences than anyone else are

    5.____

    A. Bloom and Deegan
    B. Bloom, Deegan, and Jergens
    C. Deegan and Jergens
    D. Deegan, Jergens, and O'Shea

KEY (CORRECT ANSWERS)

1. A
2. D
3. C
4. B
5. B

TEST 6

Questions 1-7.

DIRECTIONS: Questions 1 through 7 are to be answered SOLELY on the basis of the time sheet and instructions given below.

	MON.	TUBS.	WED.	THURS .	FRI.
	IN OUT	IN OUT	IN OUT	IN OUT	IN OUT
Walker	8:45 5:02	9:20 5:00	9:00 5:02	Annual Lv.	9:04 5:05
Jones	9:01 5:00	9:03 5:02	9:08 5:01	8:55 5:04	9:00 5:00
Rubins	8:49 5:04	Sick Lv.	9:05 5:04	9:03 5:03	9:04 3:30(PB)
Brown	9:00 5:01	8:55 5:03	9:00 5:05	9:04 5:07	9:05 5:03
Roberts	9:30 5:08 (PA)	8:43 5:07	9:05 5:05	9:09 12:30 (PB)	8:58 5:04

The above time sheet indicates the arrival and leaving times of five telephone operators who punched a time clock in a city agency for the week of April 14. The times they arrived at work in the mornings are indicated in the columns labeled *IN* and the times they left work are indicated in the columns labeled *OUT*. The letters (PA) mean prearranged lateness, and the letters (PB) mean personal business. Time lost for these purposes is charged to annual leave.

The operators are scheduled to arrive at 9:00. However, they are not considered late unless they arrive after 9:05. If they prearrange a lateness, they are not considered late. Time lost through lateness is charged to annual leave. A full day's work is eight hours, from 9:00 to 5:00.

1. Which operator worked the entire week WITHOUT using any annual leave or sick leave time?

    A. Jones   B. Brown
    C. Roberts   D. None of the above

1.___

2. On which days was NONE of the operators considered late?

    A. Monday and Wednesday   B. Monday and Friday
    C. Wednesday and Thursday   D. Wednesday and Friday

2.___

3. Which operator clocked out at a different time each day of the week?

    A. Roberts   B. Jones   C. Rubins   D. Brown

3.___

4. How many of the operators were considered late on Wednesday?

    A. 0   B. 1   C. 2   D. 3

4.___

5. What was the TOTAL number of charged latenesses for the week of April 14?

    A. 1   B. 3   C. 5   D. 7

5.___

6. Which day shows the MOST time charged to all types of leave by all the operators?

    A. Monday   B. Tuesday   C. Wednesday   D. Thursday

6.___

7. What operators were considered ON TIME all week?   7._____

     A. Jones and Rubins   B. Rubins and Brown
     C. Brown and Roberts   D. Walker and Brown

KEY (CORRECT ANSWERS)

1. B
2. B
3. A
4. B
5. B
6. D
7. B

TEST 7

Questions 1-10.

DIRECTIONS: Questions 1 through 10 are to be answered SOLELY on the basis of the information and code tables given below.

In accordance with these code tables, each employee in the department is assigned a
code number consisting of ten digits arranged from left to right in the following order:

I.   Division in Which Employed
II.   Title of Position
III. Annual Salary
IV.   Age
V.   Number of Years Employed in Department

EXAMPLE: A clerk is 21 years old, has been employed in the department for three years,
and is working in the Supply Division at a yearly salary of $25,000. His code number is
90-115-13-02-2.

DEPARTMENTAL CODE

TABLE I		TABLE II		TABLE III		TABLE IV		TABLE V	
Code	Division No. in Which Employed	Code	Title No. of Position	Code	Annual No. Salary	Code	No. Age	Code	No. of No. Years Employee in Dept.
10	Accounting	115	Clerk	11	$18,000 or less	01	Under 20 yrs.	1	Less than 1 yr.
20	Construc tion	155	Typist	12	$18,001 to $24,000	02	20 to 29 yrs.	2	1 to 5 yrs.
30	Engineering	175	Steno- grapher			03	30 to 39 yrs.		
40	Information	237	Book- keeper	13	$24,001 to $30,000	04	40 to 49 yrs.	3	6 to 10 yrs.
50	Maintenance	345	Statis- tician	14	$30,001 to $36,000	05	50 to 59 yrs.	4	11 to 15 yrs.
60	Personnel	545	Store- keeper			06	60 to 69 yrs.	5	16 to 25 yrs.
70	Record	633	Drafts- man	15	$36,001 to $45,000	07	70 yrs. or over	6	26 to 35 yrs.
80	Research	665	Civil Engi- neer	16	$45,001 to $60,000			7	36 yrs. or over
90	Supply	865	Machi- nist	17	$60,001 to $70,000				
		915	Porter	18	$70,001 or over				

1. A draftsman employed in the Engineering Division at a yearly salary of $34,800 is 36   1.____
    years old and has been employed in the department for 9 years.
    He should be coded

    A. 20-633-13-04-3   B. 30-865-13-03-4
    C. 20-665-14-04-4   D. 30-633-14-03-3

2. A porter employed in the Maintenance Division at a yearly salary of $28,800 is 52 years   2.____
    old and has been employed in the department for 6 years.
    He should be coded

    A. 50-915-12-03-3   B. 90-545-12-05-3
    C. 50-915-13-05-3   D. 90-545-13-03-3

3. Richard White, who has been employed in the department for 12 years, receives $50,000   3.____
    a year as a civil engineer in the Construction Division. He is 38 years old.
    He should be coded

    A. 20-665-16-03-4   B. 20-665-15-02-1
    C. 20-633-14-04-2   D. 20-865-15-02-5

4. An 18-year-old clerk appointed to the department six months ago is assigned to the   4.____
    Record Division. His annual salary is $21,600.
    He should be coded

    A. 70-115-11-01-1   B. 70-115-12-01-1
    C. 70-115-12-02-1   D. 70-155-12-01-1

5. An employee has been coded 40-155-12-03-3.   5.____
    Of the following statements regarding this employee, the MOST accurate one is that
    he is

    A. a clerk who has been employed in the department for at least 6 years
    B. a typist who receives an annual salary which does not exceed $24,000
    C. under 30 years of age and has been employed in the department for at least 11
        years
    D. employed in the Supply Division at a salary which exceeds $18,000 per annum

6. Of the following statements regarding an employee who is coded 60-175-13-01-2, the   6.____
    LEAST accurate statement is that this employee

    A. is a stenographer in the Personnel Division
    B. has been employed in the department for at least one year
    C. receives an annual salary which exceeds $24,000
    D. is more than 20 years of age

7. The following are the names of four employees of the department with their code num-   7.____
    bers:
                James Black, 80-345-15-03-4
                William White, 30-633-14-03-4
                Sam Green, 80-115-12-02-3
                John Jones, 10-237-13-04-5
    If a salary increase is to be given to the employees who have been employed in the
    department for 11 years or more and who earn less than $36,001 a year, the two of the
    above employees who will receive a salary increase are

A. John Jones and William White
B. James Black and Sam Green
C. James Black and William White
D. John Jones and Sam Green

8. Code number 50-865-14-02-6, which has been assigned to a machinist, contains an obvious inconsistency.
This inconsistency involves the figures   8.___

    A. 50-865   B. 865-14   C. 14-02   D. 02-6

9. Ten employees were awarded merit prizes for outstanding service during the year. Their code numbers were: 9.___

                80-345-14-04-4   40-155-12-02-2
                40-155-12-04-4   10-115-12-02-2
                10-115-13-03-2   80-115-13-02-2
                80-175-13-05-5   10-115-13-02-3
                10-115-12-04-3   30-633-14-04-4

Of these outstanding employees, the number who were clerks employed in the Accounting Division at a salary ranging from $24,001 to $30,000 per annum is

    A. I   B. 2   C. 3   D. 4

10. The MOST accurate of the following statements regarding the ten outstanding employees listed in the previous question is that   10.___

    A. fewer than half of the employees were under 40 years of age
    B. there were fewer typists than stenographers
    C. four of the employees were employed in the department 11 years or more
    D. two of the employees in the Research Division receive annual salaries ranging from $30,001 to $36,000

KEY (CORRECT ANSWERS)

    1. B
    2. C
    3. A
    4. B
    5. B
    6. D
    7. A
    8. D
    9. B
  10. C

ANSWER SHEET

ST NO. _____ PART _____ TITLE OF POSITION _____

(AS GIVEN IN EXAMINATION ANNOUNCEMENT - INCLUDE OPTION, IF ANY)

ACE OF EXAMINATION _____ DATE____ _____

(CITY OR TOWN)   (STATE)

RATING

USE THE SPECIAL PENCIL.   MAKE GLOSSY BLACK MARKS.

Make only ONE mark for each answer.   Additional and stray marks may be
counted as mistakes.   In making corrections, erase errors COMPLETELY.

ANSWER SHEET

TEST NO. _____ PART _____ TITLE OF POSITION _____

PLACE OF EXAMINATION _____ DATE_____

(CITY OR TOWN)   (STATE)

RATING

USE THE SPECIAL PENCIL. MAKE GLOSSY BLACK MARKS.

	A B C D E		A B C D E		A B C D E		A B C D E		A B C D E
1	⋮⋮⋮⋮⋮	26	⋮⋮⋮⋮⋮	51	⋮⋮⋮⋮⋮	76	⋮⋮⋮⋮⋮	101	⋮⋮⋮⋮⋮
2	⋮⋮⋮⋮⋮	27	⋮⋮⋮⋮⋮	52	⋮⋮⋮⋮⋮	77	⋮⋮⋮⋮⋮	102	⋮⋮⋮⋮⋮
3	⋮⋮⋮⋮⋮	28	⋮⋮⋮⋮⋮	53	⋮⋮⋮⋮⋮	78	⋮⋮⋮⋮⋮	103	⋮⋮⋮⋮⋮
4	⋮⋮⋮⋮⋮	29	⋮⋮⋮⋮⋮	54	⋮⋮⋮⋮⋮	79	⋮⋮⋮⋮⋮	104	⋮⋮⋮⋮⋮
5	⋮⋮⋮⋮⋮	30	⋮⋮⋮⋮⋮	55	⋮⋮⋮⋮⋮	80	⋮⋮⋮⋮⋮	105	⋮⋮⋮⋮⋮
6	⋮⋮⋮⋮⋮	31	⋮⋮⋮⋮⋮	56	⋮⋮⋮⋮⋮	81	⋮⋮⋮⋮⋮	106	⋮⋮⋮⋮⋮
7	⋮⋮⋮⋮⋮	32	⋮⋮⋮⋮⋮	57	⋮⋮⋮⋮⋮	82	⋮⋮⋮⋮⋮	107	⋮⋮⋮⋮⋮
8	⋮⋮⋮⋮⋮	33	⋮⋮⋮⋮⋮	58	⋮⋮⋮⋮⋮	83	⋮⋮⋮⋮⋮	108	⋮⋮⋮⋮⋮
9	⋮⋮⋮⋮⋮	34	⋮⋮⋮⋮⋮	59	⋮⋮⋮⋮⋮	84	⋮⋮⋮⋮⋮	109	⋮⋮⋮⋮⋮
10	⋮⋮⋮⋮⋮	35	⋮⋮⋮⋮⋮	60	⋮⋮⋮⋮⋮	85	⋮⋮⋮⋮⋮	110	⋮⋮⋮⋮⋮

Make only ONE mark for each answer. Additional and stray marks may be
counted as mistakes. In making corrections, erase errors COMPLETELY.

	A B C D E		A B C D E		A B C D E		A B C D E		A B C D E
11	⋮⋮⋮⋮⋮	36	⋮⋮⋮⋮⋮	61	⋮⋮⋮⋮⋮	86	⋮⋮⋮⋮⋮	111	⋮⋮⋮⋮⋮
12	⋮⋮⋮⋮⋮	37	⋮⋮⋮⋮⋮	62	⋮⋮⋮⋮⋮	87	⋮⋮⋮⋮⋮	112	⋮⋮⋮⋮⋮
13	⋮⋮⋮⋮⋮	38	⋮⋮⋮⋮⋮	63	⋮⋮⋮⋮⋮	88	⋮⋮⋮⋮⋮	113	⋮⋮⋮⋮⋮
14	⋮⋮⋮⋮⋮	39	⋮⋮⋮⋮⋮	64	⋮⋮⋮⋮⋮	89	⋮⋮⋮⋮⋮	114	⋮⋮⋮⋮⋮
15	⋮⋮⋮⋮⋮	40	⋮⋮⋮⋮⋮	65	⋮⋮⋮⋮⋮	90	⋮⋮⋮⋮⋮	115	⋮⋮⋮⋮⋮
16	⋮⋮⋮⋮⋮	41	⋮⋮⋮⋮⋮	66	⋮⋮⋮⋮⋮	91	⋮⋮⋮⋮⋮	116	⋮⋮⋮⋮⋮
17	⋮⋮⋮⋮⋮	42	⋮⋮⋮⋮⋮	67	⋮⋮⋮⋮⋮	92	⋮⋮⋮⋮⋮	117	⋮⋮⋮⋮⋮
18	⋮⋮⋮⋮⋮	43	⋮⋮⋮⋮⋮	68	⋮⋮⋮⋮⋮	93	⋮⋮⋮⋮⋮	118	⋮⋮⋮⋮⋮
19	⋮⋮⋮⋮⋮	44	⋮⋮⋮⋮⋮	69	⋮⋮⋮⋮⋮	94	⋮⋮⋮⋮⋮	119	⋮⋮⋮⋮⋮
20	⋮⋮⋮⋮⋮	45	⋮⋮⋮⋮⋮	70	⋮⋮⋮⋮⋮	95	⋮⋮⋮⋮⋮	120	⋮⋮⋮⋮⋮
21	⋮⋮⋮⋮⋮	46	⋮⋮⋮⋮⋮	71	⋮⋮⋮⋮⋮	96	⋮⋮⋮⋮⋮	121	⋮⋮⋮⋮⋮
22	⋮⋮⋮⋮⋮	47	⋮⋮⋮⋮⋮	72	⋮⋮⋮⋮⋮	97	⋮⋮⋮⋮⋮	122	⋮⋮⋮⋮⋮
23	⋮⋮⋮⋮⋮	48	⋮⋮⋮⋮⋮	73	⋮⋮⋮⋮⋮	98	⋮⋮⋮⋮⋮	123	⋮⋮⋮⋮⋮
24	⋮⋮⋮⋮⋮	49	⋮⋮⋮⋮⋮	74	⋮⋮⋮⋮⋮	99	⋮⋮⋮⋮⋮	124	⋮⋮⋮⋮⋮
25	⋮⋮⋮⋮⋮	50	⋮⋮⋮⋮⋮	75	⋮⋮⋮⋮⋮	100	⋮⋮⋮⋮⋮	125	⋮⋮⋮⋮⋮